The *Best*
Is Yet to Come

The *Best* Is Yet to Come

7 DOORS OF SPIRITUAL GROWTH

John H. Kieschnick

Author photographs by Rebecca Snedecor Musso, Visions & Vogue, Houston, Texas

Cover photography by Joel Endicott, Gloria Dei Lutheran Church, Houston, Texas

Front cover design by Joe Gonzalez-Reinhart, Gloria Dei Lutheran Church, Houston, Texas

Formatting and dust jacket design by Anne McLaughlin, Blue Lake Design, Dickinson, Texas

Images of doors on pages 10, 68, 94, 118, 156, 180, 202 © iStockPhoto.com; images of doors on pages 20, 46, 138 © Artville

Published in the United States by Baxter Press, Friendswood, Texas

ISBN: 1-888237-65-1

This book is dedicated to...

. . . my beautiful wife, Elaine, and our three wonderful children, Jonathan, Kimberly and Jason, who have been special evidences of God's grace to me, and
. . . the people of Gloria Dei Lutheran Church, who have greatly enriched my life by extending God's grace to me time and again, and who have joined me in believing that "the best is yet to come."

Table of Contents

Acknowledgments 9

Introduction: Open Doors 11

Chapter 1   Jesus: Behind Every Door 21

Chapter 2   Witness: The Door of Opportunity 47

Chapter 3   Worship: The Door of Wonder 69

Chapter 4   Connections: The Door of Encouragement 95

Chapter 5   Prayer: The Door of Intimacy 119

Chapter 6   Bible Study: The Door of Insight 139

Chapter 7   Service: The Door of Fulfillment 157

Chapter 8   Giving: The Door of Authentic Faith 181

Chapter 9   Growth: Walking through the Doors 203

Endnotes   223

Appendices

    About the Author 225

    How to Lead a Group or Class Using
    The Best Is Yet to Come 229

    The Spiritual Health Awareness Survey 233

    To Order More Books 239

Acknowledgments

This book is the result of input from many different individuals who have contributed first to enrich my life, and then to create and produce this book. I would like to thank…

The people of Gloria Dei Lutheran Church (GDLC), with whom I have been privileged to share a partnership in the grace of God for over 30 years.

The GDLC staff who originally challenged me to write this book and the Board of Directors who took the risk to have it published. Without their encouragement and support, the message of this book could never have been lived or written.

My Friday morning accountability group of men who have prayed regularly for me and have stood faithfully by me through thick and thin.

Pat Springle of Baxter Press who has so beautifully crafted into written words so many of my verbal comments which comprise the heart of this book.

Vince Parks, GDLC's Executive Director of Ministry, who spent countless hours encouraging, challenging, and supporting me in this effort.

Betty McIntyre, my Administrative Assistant, for her assistance with the manuscript.

Michelle Gooding, one of GDLC's administrative assistants, who served as the primary proofreader.

My wife, Elaine, who is my toughest critic, my steadfast companion, and my partner in pursuing Jesus with our whole hearts.

The God and Father of my Lord Jesus Christ, who has blessed me in the heavenly realms with every spiritual blessing in Christ and enables me to believe with certainty that "the best is yet to come."

Introduction

OPEN DOORS

"'For I know the plans I have for you,' declares the Lord, 'plans to prosper you and not to harm you, plans to give you hope and a future'" (Jeremiah 29:11).

"For many of us the great danger is not that we will renounce our faith. It is that we will become so distracted and rushed and preoccupied that we will settle for a mediocre version of it."
—John Ortberg

*W*hen I open a door, I always have a sense of anticipation. I vividly remember Christmas in our family when I was a little boy. I was the second youngest of nine children, and on Christmas morning, my parents made us stand outside the living room where they had put all the presents. The door was closed, and in those wonderful moments before my dad opened the door, we anticipated all we'd find on the other side of that door. With wide eyes and excited voices, we jabbered to each other about the bicycle or doll or game we hoped we'd get. Today, those memories of shared anticipation behind the door with my brothers and sisters are more precious than any gift we received.

I also remember the first home Elaine and I bought years ago. Like any young couple, we longed for a home of our own. We talked and planned and dreamed about it, and we looked for a long time to find just the right home in which to raise our family. One day, we walked through the door of a small house of less than 1250 square feet. We looked at each other, and we instantly knew, "This is it!" That house was everything we hoped it would be, and I cherish the memories of our life there.

Doors open to opportunities. They may be as obvious as a wedding, a newborn baby, a new job, or we may be totally unaware of them because our senses have been numbed by the humdrum routine of life. I believe all of us have far more God-given potential than we've ever dreamed possible, and doors of opportunity are in front of us every day . . . even for me. I recall the excitement of new opportunities when I was a young man. In those days, everything was a challenge! But even today as a "seasoned veteran," I have a clear, strong sense that God isn't finished with me yet. He has more for me to accomplish and more for me to experience. I'm just as eager today as I was when I left school and at each turning point in my family life and career. For each of us, I truly believe the best is yet to come.

THE ADVENTURE

Don't misunderstand me. The "best" that God gives us isn't an unbroken climb up the road of success. As Carrie ten Boom once observed, "Faith is a fantastic adventure in trusting him." Taking God's hand is the most exciting and wonderful adventure we can ever experience, but it's a challenge, and sometimes, more challenge than we want. Adventures always involve risks, and walking with Jesus is no exception. He takes us through the most joyous moments life can offer, but inevitably, he also leads us through times of darkness and confusion. If we examine the path of Jesus' life, we won't be surprised by the ups and downs in the journey as we walk with him and cling to his hand. Think of the disciples on the afternoon of Good Friday when the one they followed was dead and being carried to a tomb. That certainly didn't seem like a door of opportunity! But the pain, confusion, and discouragement they

> **Adventures always involve risks, and walking with Jesus is no exception.**

faced that day were washed away in the flood of joy they experienced when they saw the glorified Jesus, alive and well, just a few days later.

The ultimate thrill ride is to take Jesus' hand and walk with him through every door of opportunity and challenge he brings our way. Sometimes, we'll enter those doors with the biggest smile in the world, but sometimes, we'll face real hardships and be tempted to run away. Christ's goal is not to make life easy for us; it's to deepen our dependence on him. Knowing his love, forgiveness, and strength through thick and thin thrills our hearts and fills us with hope. As we sense his kindness and discover his purposes, we'll be convinced that the best truly is yet to come. Martin Luther knew the importance of responding boldly to the grace of God. He observed, "Faith is a living, daring confidence in God's grace, so sure and certain that a man could stake his life on it a thousand times."

STARTING POINTS

Today, many people examine the claims of Jesus because they know deep in their gut that there has to be more to life. Some are trying to fill the hole in their hearts with corporate success, some with possessions, and some are just "raising hell" to give themselves a thrill. But in their quiet, reflective moments, they long for something that really satisfies. That something is a someone. His name is Jesus.

I meet with many men and women, young and old, who are new to the faith, and they also sense that they are missing something. They've tasted the goodness of God, and they've gotten their feet wet in his grace and power. Now, they want to dive into the deep end of the pool!

Some others (and I was one of them a few years ago) have done "the church thing" so long that it has become stale. They still go through the motions, but God's kingdom looks less and less inviting to them. I recall talking with some men from my church who had struggled with temptations to abandon their faith and their families because they felt bone-tired and deeply discouraged. One of them wondered out loud if he'd be happier if he had an affair. One of his friends looked at him intently and said, "Brother, you're taking a step on a slippery slope. I know times are tough right now, but I assure you, having an affair is *not* the door to an abundant life!" When we are tired and discouraged, thoughts drift, and eventually, behavior that was once unthinkable becomes a thought, then an option, and maybe even a plan.

Countless others have settled for a bland, lifeless form of Christianity. They sing the songs and hear the messages, but they are distracted by the cares of living. They once had a burning love for God, but over the years, that flame has died and is now only an ember. They still feel close to God from time to time, but these are fleeting moments. They used to make bold decisions to speak out for Christ, give sacrificially, and meet needs wherever they found them, but now, they just go through the motions of attending worship most Sundays, giving a little out of their surplus, and are no longer excited about the ministries of the church. Still, the ember is there. If exposed to a little fuel and oxygen, I believe these people can flame again!

> **If exposed to a little fuel and oxygen, I believe these people can flame again!**

DOORS AND GRACE

In these pages, we'll look at seven doors of spiritual growth: witness, worship, connections with other believers, prayer, Bible study, service, and giving. However, please understand right now that these are not techniques for a better life. They are ways to connect more deeply to the one who is the source of life. We don't participate in these disciplines *to get* grace or God's favor. We pursue them *because we've experienced* God's amazing grace and want to know him better. Throughout each chapter, we'll examine the implications of God's incredible grace in each of

14

these pursuits. His love and forgiveness is the foundation of our spiritual lives, and they sustain us in every step of growth. There are many motivations to live for Christ, but all of them come back to a deep, rich, awe-filled gratitude that the God of the universe, who needed nothing and no one, stooped to express his love in a way that obliterated the barrier of sin that separated us from him. Today, I marvel more than ever before at his grace. And in many ways, this sense of wonder assures me that the best really is yet to come—in this life and in the one beyond.

Many of us sense that God is opening the door of a new, rich, challenging life for us, and we're eager to open that door and walk in. But for any number of reasons, some of us only tiptoe up to the door and crack it an inch or two. We are afraid of what we'll find on the other side. I love C. S. Lewis' *Chronicles of Narnia,* and one of my favorite moments is in the first book of the series, *The Lion, the Witch, and the Wardrobe.* Mrs. Beaver tells Lucy about Aslan, the elusive lion of Narnia, who is a Christ-figure in the stories. Mrs. Beaver tells the little girl of Aslan's power and majesty and how he sometimes appears in times of trouble. Little Lucy feels overwhelmed with the thought that she might someday actually face this awesome beast. She asks timidly, "Is he safe?"

"Oh no, dearie," Mrs. Beaver almost laughs at the thought. "He's not safe. But he's good."

Jesus is a person, awesome and tender, majestic and kind. He leads us "in paths of righteousness," but those paths are through valleys as well as on mountaintops. Like Lucy, we may be timid because we aren't sure if he's safe, but we can cling to him because we're sure that he is, indeed, good.

EVERY DOOR

I believe God is behind every door, and he delights in us when we open those doors and walk through boldly. He stands behind every door to meet us, greet us, confront us, change us, mold us, and transform us. He wants to make us more like Jesus.

The doors of opportunity and challenge necessarily involve changes in attitudes, behavior, and direction. Change, though, can be threatening. Years ago, my staff and I were going through some big changes, and we experienced some very difficult struggles. I asked a counselor to help me sort out all the confusion. After listening to me for a while, he told me, "John, you love change . . . until it impacts *you.*" I've never forgotten his insight. Most people know me as a man who takes bold steps of faith, but in my heart, I fear change like everyone else. I was happy for God to change my staff, my leaders, my wife, and my kids, but that day, I realized that God wanted to do his work in me. He wanted to change me, too.

Walking through God's doors of opportunity and challenge has brought the most fulfillment I've ever experienced, and thankfully, I have those experiences quite often. One of my favorite passages of Scripture captures this sense of deep satisfaction. Jesus had taken his men a long way out of the way to travel through Samaria. On a hot, dusty day at about noon, the disciples went to town to find something to eat, but Jesus stayed near Jacob's well. Soon, a woman came to draw water. Jesus initiated a conversation with her, and in the course of a few minutes, he exposed her need for forgiveness and grace. To others, she was a three-time loser. She was a Samaritan (Samaritans were despised by the Jews), she was an outcast because of her sexual escapades, and she was a woman (women weren't respected in that culture). But where others saw shame and fear, Jesus saw a person who needed his grace. As they talked, He opened the door, and she trusted in him.

When the disciples came back with some food, they were shocked that Jesus was talking with the Samaritan woman. Soon, she left to tell everybody in town about Jesus. The disciples turned to him and asked him if he wanted something to eat. Jesus no doubt smiled at his friends and shook his head. He felt full, he said, but not because he had eaten. He felt deep contentment because he had responded to the Father's will and touched a life.

"My food," he told them, "is to do the will of him who sent me" (John 4:34). When I respond to God's invitation and open doors of opportunity and challenge, I know exactly what Jesus was talking about because I, too, feel that deepest sense of satisfaction.

The good news is that no matter who you are, no matter what you've done, and no matter where you've been, God is standing behind a door calling your name. It's not too late. He's waiting for you to respond, however timidly or boldly, to his gracious invitation. And he's not looking for perfect people. In the four life stories of Jesus, called the gospels, we find Jesus extending his hand to prostitutes and lepers, tax collectors and church officials, women and children, the sick, the demon possessed, the rich, the poor, Jews and Gentiles—everyone! He invited each of them, and he invites each of us, to experience his love, forgiveness, and strength. And he says, "I'll make your life more meaningful than you ever dreamed! The best, I assure you, is yet to come."

> **He's waiting for you to respond, however timidly or boldly, to his gracious invitation.**

The title of this book has a two-fold meaning. When we think about the future, we naturally focus on the next few years of our lives. But God's best is not limited. If we take his hand and trust him, the doors of opportunity and challenge open for us every day throughout our lives . . . and beyond. You see, even though I'm getting older—more mature, if you will—I'm really excited about experiencing God's best for me today, tomorrow, and for the rest of my life. But that's not the half of it. Someday, when I take my last breath, I'll wake up in the presence of Jesus and begin an eternity of new opportunities and challenges, not encumbered by sin, not limited by time, and not clouded by doubt. The very best, then, will be a reality! The Scriptures indicate that what I do today will make a difference then. On that day, I want to hear Jesus say to me, "Well done, good and faithful servant. Enter into the joy of your Master." That will be a great day!

MAKING A DIFFERENCE

I hope that God will use this book in your life to deepen your grasp of his grace and transform you more into the image of his Son. Actually, that's what I hope he does in my life, too. As I began writing, I told Elaine that I wanted God to touch me more deeply than ever before. I want to gain a deeper appreciation for all God has done for me so that my life overflows in gratitude. I want God to use this book to make a difference in your life, but I'm convinced that he first wants to make a difference in me.

Reading articles and books stimulates my thinking and teaches me important principles, but I've found that pointed questions and honest conversations with friends help me apply those principles in my own experience. Perhaps you will, too. In this book, each "Think About It" section at the end of the chapters contains a few questions to guide your reflection and application. After that, I've added a few additional questions to help you go deeper.

We've provided some space for you to write your answers, but you will need a separate notebook if you want to write more. Use these questions to reflect, pray, and consider how God wants to fill your life with his grace so that his love, forgiveness, and power overflow into all your relationships and actions. These questions are also designed to stimulate rich, meaningful discussions in small groups.

At the end of this introduction, I want to ask just a few questions to get you started.

THINK ABOUT IT

1. What are some doors of opportunity God might be opening in your life right now? What are some doors of challenge?

2. What might be some doors that you need to close or that need to stay closed? Explain your answer.

3. Read Jeremiah 29:11. What difference does it make to you that the plans for hope and prosperity are from the Lord, not of your own design?

4. What do you hope to get out of reading and reflecting on this book?

1 · Jesus

BEHIND EVERY DOOR

". . . in order that in the coming ages he might show the incomparable riches of his grace, expressed in kindness to us in Christ Jesus" (Ephesians 2:7).

"As long as I am constantly concerned about what I 'ought' to say, think, do or feel, I am still the victim of my surroundings and not liberated. . . . But when I can accept my identity from God and allow Him to be the center of my life, I am liberated from compulsion and can move without restraints." — Henri Nouwen

Jesus amazed people. He said and did things that caused people to marvel. John's gospel records seven miraculous "signs" that proved Jesus was the long awaited Messiah, and John included a number of conversations in which Jesus told people who he was. Over and over again in his account, John tells us that when they encountered Jesus, people wondered about him and asked, "Who *is* this man?"

In one of these conversations, Jesus used the metaphor of shepherding to explain his role. He told them he was "the good shepherd," and "the door" for sheep who want to come to God (John 10:7-18). Jesus' words weren't idle conversation—his statements astounded them. To grasp the power and shock of his message, we have to understand the Jewish culture. His simple statement, "I am the door," demanded a response from those who listened to him. He wasn't saying that he had hinges and a handle. In this and several other "I am" statements, Jesus was claiming to be God himself. The people who listened to him that day knew the story of Moses like the back of their hands. A Hebrew boy rescued from the Nile as an infant by Pharaoh's daughter, Moses grew up as a prince of Egypt. As a man, he learned that he was a Jew, just like the slaves who labored to build monuments to the Pharaoh. In a fit of rage, Moses murdered an Egyptian slave master, and then fled to the wilderness where he spent forty years virtually alone. One day, God revealed himself to Moses in a burning bush and commanded him to go back to Egypt to free the Hebrew slaves. Years in the desert hadn't deadened Moses sharp mind. He imagined the scene of demanding "in God's name" that Pharaoh free his kinsmen, and he wanted to have as much authority as possible. He knew he would need a vital piece of information: the name of God. Prostrate before the burning bush and God's awesome presence, Moses asked, "Who can I say sent me?"

God told him to tell them he was sent by "I Am Who I Am." In doing so he declared that the one who sent him was the eternal, pre-existent, almighty God (Exodus 3:13-15).

When Jesus said, *"I am* the door," those who heard him that day understood that he was claiming to be the same God as the one who spoke to Moses!

When Jesus said, *"I am* the door," those who heard him that day understood that he was claiming to be the same God as the one who spoke to Moses! We know they grasped the significance of his claim because some thought he was demon-possessed, some wondered if he was insane, and others believed in him. We find the same range of responses to Jesus' claims today.

WONDER AND MYSTERY

The Christian life is not about rules, regulations, and rituals. It's about a person. Certainly, the traditions and sacraments of the church are meaningful, but only and always if they flow out of a sense of wonder and gratitude for Christ himself. In our day, as it was in the early church, people have difficulty embracing both the divinity and humanity of Christ. It's far easier to say he was God but not human or human but not God. Even in the early church, though, leaders made it crystal clear that he was, in fact, both. John tells us in his prologue that the eternal Word "became flesh and made his dwelling among us" (John 1:14), and Paul explains in beautiful poetry that Christ, "being in very nature God, . . . made himself nothing, taking the very nature of a servant" and died a horrible death for us (Philippians 2:6-11).

Jesus created the incredible expanse of the universe and is "far above all," yet he calls you and me his "friends." Theologians call the unique blend of his humanity and divinity the *hypostatic union,* and they say that he is both *transcendent* and *immanent.* These terms aren't just great church words or for games of Scrabble. They explode our pitifully small preconceptions of the nature of God and give us a profound sense of wonder and mystery. These concepts are the essence of faith.

> They explode our pitifully small preconceptions of the nature of God and give us a profound sense of wonder and mystery.

Throughout history, people have felt uncomfortable with things they can't fully comprehend and things they can't control. God, by his very nature, is beyond anything we can fathom, and we are fools if we think we can control him. The apostle John was perhaps Jesus' best friend on earth. In his gospel, he calls himself "the disciple Jesus loved." Does that mean Jesus only loved him and not the others? Certainly not. But the love of Jesus was so rich and real to John that it completely dominated his sense of identity. It was John who, at the Last Supper, laid his head on Jesus' chest. In the opening chapter of the Revelation, the risen Christ appears in a vision of glory to his friend John. The image was so overwhelming that John "fell at his feet as though dead." John fainted!

I often ask myself, "How do I respond to Jesus? Do I have a sense of wonder and mystery at his incomparable greatness and kindness toward me?"

People ask—or at least they want to ask—some tough questions, such as:

- What will I gain if I follow Jesus, and what will I lose if I don't?

- Does it make sense to live for someone I can't even see, instead of focusing all my resources on tangible things I can see and thoroughly enjoy?

- How can I fulfill the minimum standards for God and get by without shaking up my life too much?

These are just a few of the questions people instinctively ask about the Christian life. Jesus answered these by asking one himself: "What good will it be for a man if he gains the whole world, yet forfeits his soul?" (Matthew 16:26) The visible, tangible things try to seduce us, but God has made us so that only he can ultimately satisfy our deepest real need. Far too often, we settle for lesser gods of success, pleasure, and approval. Every advertisement on television, in magazines, in newspapers, on billboards, and in all other media promises that these things will bring us happiness, contentment, and thrills. And they might . . . for a moment. But the incessant pursuit of these things isn't merely an enticing diversion—it's sin. If we excuse or rationalize our heart's preoccupation with

> **But the incessant pursuit of these things isn't merely an enticing diversion—it's sin.**

these lesser gods, we'll become numb to the things of God, or worse, we'll try to use him to help us get more success, pleasure, and approval. That, I'm convinced, is the idolatry of our age.

When we try to use Christ to fulfill our own selfish wants, we reduce God to our personal servant. Author and psychologist Larry Crabb observes that many of us think of God as "a specially attentive waiter."[1] When we get good service from him, we give him a nice tip of thanks and praise. When we don't get what we want, we whine and complain.

Jesus isn't a waiter who does whatever we ask, and he isn't an impersonal vending machine who dispenses blessings if we say or do exactly the right things. If we have even the slightest glimpse of the awesome wonder and incredible kindness of Jesus Christ, we will see the stark contrast between him and our lesser gods. That insight reveals our need for forgiveness and compels us to want to please the one who died for us.

DESPERATE NEED

In the last generation or so, pop psychologists have seen the despair in people's lives and offered a solution. They say that focusing on our innate goodness can rectify "a poor self-concept." A host of models, theories, and practices tell us, "I'm OK. You're OK" and demand tolerance of other religions and other lifestyles. These messages pervade our schools and media, but people are just as devastated today as they were a few years ago, if not more so, because the root problem is not being addressed.

In a seminal work several decades ago, Dr. Karl Menninger asked, *Whatever Became of Sin?* Menninger's research tracked the declining recognition of sin as the central problem of humanity. He noted that our culture feels completely uncomfortable with personal responsibility, so we blame our selfish, destructive behavior on our parents, on society, and on anyone else other than ourselves. People don't "sin" today, he notes, they have "issues." Their addictions aren't the result of poor personal choices—they are "sick." Stealing and murder are social problems to be handled by the judicial system, not through personal responsibility and repentance. He asked, "Does that mean that no sin is involved in all our troubles—sin with an 'I' in the middle? Is no one any longer guilty of anything? Guilty perhaps of a sin that could be repented and repaired and atoned for? Is it only that someone may be stupid or sick or criminal—or asleep?"[2]

Amazing advances in medicine and technology have made life easier, but I fear these steps forward come at an unintended expense. Many people now believe that doctors, engineers, and inventors can solve all problems. Life, we've become convinced, should be easy and pleasant. We avoid serious personal reflection—and especially the admission of guilt—at all costs. In his insightful and challenging book, *A Nation of Victims,* author Charles Sykes notes that today virtually every grievance is litigated, not grieved and forgiven so that relationships can be restored.

> **The door to grace, however, is a deep grasp of our desperate need for a Savior.**

The door to grace, however, is a deep grasp of our desperate need for a Savior. We aren't "basically good people" who need just a few more pep talks to help us realize how good we are. We are helpless, hopeless sinners, far away from God and with no possible way of earning his love, forgiveness, and acceptance.

LAW AND GOSPEL

Some might say, "Stop, Pastor K. You're way too harsh. Tell us about God's love, not sin." Ah, friends, you misunderstand. Grace has no meaning apart from sin and judgment. Mercy can be defined as "not getting what we deserve," but grace goes farther: It's "getting what we don't deserve." The Scriptures tell us that we were wonderfully made by God, but we have tragically fallen into sin and separation from God. From Genesis to Revelation, we see that God, in his great grace, didn't leave us hopeless and helpless. He sent a Savior to buy us back from destruction, rescue us from judgment, and free us from slavery to sin.

Author Philip Yancey described these truths as follows: "The world is good, the world is fallen, and the world can be redeemed." He observes, "Redemption promises not replacement—a wholly new creation imposed on the old—but a transformation that somehow makes use of all that went before. We realize God's design as reclaimed originals, like a priceless oil painting restored after a fire or a cathedral rebuilt after a bombing. Redemption involves a kind of alchemy, a philosopher's stone that makes gold from clay. In the end, evil itself will serve as a tool of good."[3]

Redemption necessarily includes desperate debt and the specific price paid. Both, not one or the other. Sometimes I hear people say, "I see two Gods in the Bible. The Old Testament God is full of anger and judgment, but the New Testament God is a God of love." I cringe when I hear people say that. They obviously haven't read enough of both the Old and New Testaments to see the beautiful descriptions of God's tenderness and kindness in the Old and God's righteous wrath outlined in the New. And they obviously don't understand the crucial link between the law and the gospel. This link is essential to our grasp of grace.

The law consists of the commands of God found throughout the Bible. The Old Testament describes several categories of law for the Jewish people, but God's moral law transcends time and culture. The law isn't "sub-Christian" or "un-Christian." It reveals the perfection of God and his standards for us. Paul tells us that the law is tremendously valuable as our tutor to lead us to Christ (Galatians 3:23-25). As we read about God's righteous standards and his commands, our sins are exposed, and we realize how much we need to be forgiven!

Sadly, most people try to build their lives on the law. They try to establish their worth, their identity, their meaning in life, and their standing before God and others by what they do. They measure everything they do to establish their value so they can say, "See, I'm good enough," or "See, I'm better than you." Doing good enough or comparing favorably is their reward, but it leaves them empty because they can never be sure if they've earned enough points. This perception of life is deeply ingrained in our psyche, and it is reinforced by our culture.

I read a book many years ago titled *I Hurt Inside,* by Ralph Underwager. He made the insightful observation that all psychological pain is the result of our attempts to justify ourselves before God by what we do. The more I have thought about this, the more I'm convinced he's right. Trying to make ourselves right and acceptable to God and to others based upon our best efforts always comes up short, and in the end, we suffer great pain. God, though, has provided a much better way.

Trying to make ourselves right and acceptable to God and to others based upon our best efforts always comes up short, and in the end, we suffer great pain.

In a series of lectures, C. F. W. Walther detailed the distinctions and harmony of the law and the gospel. He noted, "Both are equally necessary. Apart from the Law we do not understand the Gospel, and apart from the Gospel the Law is of no use to us." The law, our concept of right and wrong, "was written in man's heart at his creation" and is pricked by his conscience. The written law, such as the Ten Commandments, was given "to restore the faded writing in the heart."[4]

Both law and gospel are gifts from God, and their ultimate goals are the same. Both are designed to lead us to salvation. The law prepares our hearts by showing us our desperate need for forgiveness, and the gospel gives us redemption in the sacrifice of Christ to pay for our sins. Luther wrote, "These two points must be made: The Law creates a thirst and leads us to hell; the Gospel, however, satisfies the thirst and leads to heaven. The Law states what we must do, but that we have fallen short of doing it, no matter how holy we may be. Thus it produces uncertainty in me and arouses this thirst."[5]

When I read that the Great Commandment is to love God with all my heart and the second is to love my neighbor as myself, my heart tells me instantly that I have failed God. I don't love him with all my heart. I care too much about what people think of me, and I'm often too preoccupied with my own desires so that I don't even notice the needs of others. I'm not surprised by this fact, so I don't try to excuse myself or rationalize my attitude. I fall short of God's standard all the time! But this realization reminds me again and again of the grace of the gospel, the wonderful cleansing of forgiveness God has given me through Jesus' sacrifice, and I can experience his grace again as I confess and repent.

THE BITTER ROOT OF SELF

Grace is radical, powerful, and beautiful. But if that's the case, why don't more people experience the transforming joy of being set free by God's grace? Years ago, I read a message by the German theologian, Helmut Thielecke. He said there are three groups of people in the world. One is a very small group of devoted atheists who are convinced God doesn't exist. On the other end of the spectrum is a small group of men and women who are completely sold out to Jesus Christ. And between the two is an enormous group of people who wish they were in one group or the other. Lukewarm Christians are miserable people. They know enough of the love and power of God to assure them they are missing God's best, but their fear prevents them from taking bold steps to embrace grace wholeheartedly. In many cases, they simply don't want to let go of the hope that they can make life work on their own. That's a tension in my own life—dependence on self instead of God—which is sheer, unadulterated, unvarnished sin.

When we say "yes" to God the first time or the millionth time, we are also saying "no" to our sinful passions that demand control and insist on taking all the credit for success. That was the sin of our first parents in the Garden, "to be like God," and it's our sin today. It still stinks in the nostrils of God.

In previous eras, pastors called this sin "self-righteousness," the attempt to justify ourselves by our right actions apart from the grace of God. In the pages of the Bible, we find three distinct types:

"I am good enough to earn God's acceptance."

Luke records Jesus' parable of the tax collector and the Pharisee (Luke 18:9-14), who both went to the temple to pray. The Pharisee reminded God of all he had done for God, and how much better he was than the sinful tax collector standing nearby. The tax collector, though, was overwhelmed with the weight of his own sin and wouldn't even lift his eyes to heaven. He beat his chest and begged God for mercy. Jesus told his listeners that the humble tax collector went away right with God, not the religious Pharisee, who did everything right and expected to win God's acceptance by his good behavior. "For everyone who exalts himself will be humbled," Jesus told them, "and he who humbles himself will be exalted."

"I know better than God what is best for me. I deserve better!"

When the psalmist Asaph looked at his own life of suffering and then at the unrighteous who enjoyed happiness and plenty, he was outraged (Psalm 73)! The law of the harvest, he demanded, should have applied to him . . . and them! The remedy for his self-righteous attitude was a fresh perspective that God's justice would prevail—someday.

"I would never act like he does!"

In Jesus' parable of the prodigal son (Luke 15:11-32), the elder brother was furious that his father restored his wayward brother to full status in the family. The defense of his attitude was, "Look! All these years I've been slaving for you and never disobeyed your orders. Yet you never gave me even a young goat so I could celebrate with my friends. But when this son of yours who has squandered your property with prostitutes comes home, you kill the fattened calf for him!" (Luke 15:29-30) The elder brother felt he was superior because he had always done the right thing, but comparison produced bitterness and prevented him from enjoying the blessings of his father's love.

All three forms of self-righteousness place demands on God. Each has the expectation of receiving better treatment in exchange for something done to "earn it." That attitude says, "Look at all I've done! I deserve to be blessed!" Self-righteousness is an attempt to put ourselves in a position so we can say (or at least believe in our hearts), "God owes me!" Instead of enjoying the love and freedom given by God, self-righteous people live by rigid, demanding, and often arbitrary rules. They measure themselves— and their value—by how many rules they haven't broken or by how well they stack up against those who have broken some (or many) rules. And in demented delight, they measure others by those same rules. When they find faults in others they feel better about themselves.

> **Self-righteousness is an attempt to put ourselves in a position so we can say (or at least believe in our hearts), "God owes me!"**

Self-righteousness holds the grace of God at a distance and refuses to acknowledge the deep, desperate need to be forgiven and cleansed of our own sinfulness. If there was ever anyone who deserved better, Paul implies in his letter to the Philippians, it is Christ. If there was ever anyone who could have rightly been angry for being treated so badly and having things turn out so wrong, it was Jesus. But he didn't gripe and complain. He loved. To the degree that we grasp the incredible gift of Christ to humble himself and die a horrible death for us—for me!—our self-righteousness will melt away.

THE RICHES OF GRACE

Many of us are familiar with the axiom that grace is "God's Riches At Christ's Expense." Allow me to amplify this thought and expand on some insights I learned from Rick Warren, pastor of Saddleback Community Church and author of *The Purpose Drive Life.*[6]

Grace is God's GIFT to us.

If you were to ask ten people, "How do you think God wants to relate to you?" and "On what basis do you think God will let you into heaven?" what would you expect them to say? When I have asked those questions, people have told me, "I try to be good." "I try to be as nice as I can." "I go to church, maybe not every Sunday, but most of the time." "I try to serve God as best I can." "I try to live a good life." But there's a problem in these responses: We can't get into heaven by what we do. We just can't be good enough to earn God's acceptance.

But there's good news: God will accept us if, and only if, we accept his gift of grace. This is the fundamental difference between Christianity and every other faith or religion. Every other religion says you must build your life on *what you do,* but Christianity is different. The Bible says you build your life, get to know God, have a relationship with him, have your sins forgiven, and go to heaven only by accepting what *God has done for you.* Grace is God's gift to you.

Grace is RECEIVED through faith.

In Ephesians 2:8-9, Paul wrote, "For it is by grace you have been saved through faith and this is not from yourselves. It is the gift of God, not by works, lest anyone should boast." Even faith is a gift from God. If you believe, it's because God gave you the faith to believe. Forgiveness, salvation, and eternal life cannot be based upon our performance, but only on God's promise. It is based on God's grace, which we receive solely through faith.

Many of us, though, feel guilty about our past, pressured about our present, and worried about our future. All of these problems have been settled by the grace of God. When grace becomes the foundation for our lives, we will discover it will hold us up through every circumstance of life.

> **When grace becomes the foundation for our lives, we will discover it will hold us up through every circumstance of life.**

Grace is AVAILABLE to all.

God doesn't play favorites. Regardless of your status, your background, or your past sins, God's grace is available to you. No matter who you are, and no matter what you've done, God wants to shower his grace on you. Before Paul became the spokesman and leader of the early church, he stood by as a mob killed Stephen, and he went all over the country to arrest and persecute believers. Then Jesus touched his life, forgave him and transformed him. God's grace was so rich and real that his letters overflow with gratitude for God's kindness and forgiveness.

Grace is CHRIST-CENTERED.

Grace only comes through Jesus Christ. He's the one who paid for it. Grace is free, but it's not cheap. It cost Christ his life. That's how expensive our relationship with God, our freedom from the slavery of sin, and our ticket to heaven was. It cost the life of Jesus Christ.

Because grace is Christ-centered, there's nothing you can do to make God love you more than he already does, and there is nothing you can do to make God love you any less. His love is based upon grace, not on your merit; on his mercy, not on your goodness.

A grasp of grace changes lives. Not long ago, a lady told me some of the struggles she had had over the years. Recently, she came to know the grace of God in Jesus Christ, and she reflected, "There's no therapy in the world, no pill, no book, and no seminar that can make the kinds of changes God's grace has made in my life."

Grace is ETERNALLY EXPERIENCED.

Most of us don't think much about eternity until someone dies, but the Bible calls us to have an eternal perspective. Paul wrote these words to the Christians in the city of Rome, "The wages of sin is death (that's the bad news), but the gift of God is eternal life through Christ Jesus our Lord (that's the good news)." The word "eternal" reminds us that grace is the gift that keeps on giving, not just in time, but also for eternity. The relationship that we begin now is one God intends for us to have with him in perfection in eternity.

One of the most brilliant men I've ever seen in video and in print was Peter Drucker, the father of American management. He was a brilliant man who knew something about everything. One day Rick Warren, pastor of Saddleback Community Church and author of *The Purpose Driven Life,* met Drucker in his home and asked him, "How is it that you finally became a Christian? What led you to affirm Jesus Christ as your Savior and Lord?"

Drucker thought for a moment and said, "When I finally understood grace, I realized I was never going to get a better deal than that."

I have often said, "I continue to be amazed at how the grace of God in Jesus Christ continues to roll over me day after day after day." And I'll experience this grace throughout eternity.

MAKING IT REAL

How do people change? Think back to Dr. Menninger's observations that the concept of personal responsibility for destructive behavior (which the Bible calls "sin") has been diluted and denied. But when we downplay the significance of sin, we find superficial solutions that simply won't touch the deepest, darkest crevasses of need in our hearts. If we call it sickness, we look for healing. If we call it a crime, we seek rehabilitation. If we say those behaviors are just issues, we hope to resolve them. If we excuse them because someone hurt us first, we remain victims instead of victors. No, sin must be forgiven. There's no other solution for it.

Some well-meaning Christians are honest about their sins, but their remedy is to "let go and let God." Change, they are certain, comes when they become passive

But when we downplay the significance of sin, we find superficial solutions that simply won't touch the deepest, darkest crevasses of need in our hearts.

and hope God changes them. I believe there are a few occasions when we have done all we can possibly do to follow God's directions, but the doors are still closed. At those moments, letting go and letting God is appropriate. But passivity is not the norm for the Christian life. In the vast majority of instances, change comes when we courageously act. For example, when God's Spirit, my wife, or a friend tells me that my attitude stinks, I have a choice. I can blow them off and continue in my sin, or I can respond like David when Nathan confronted him with his sin of adultery and murder. Nathan told the king, "Thou art the man!" And David responded with honesty and contrition, "I have sinned before the Lord." In my own moments of stark reality, I have a choice, either to deny my sin or to affirm God's forgiveness and choose a new direction.

We shouldn't be shocked when the Holy Spirit taps us on the shoulder and says, "That selfish attitude is wrong" or "That action hurt your friend, and it's sin." The Spirit's loving confrontation is the beginning of a process that makes grace real in our lives. The process is called repentance, which includes confession, absolution, and amendment.

Confession is agreeing with God. First, we agree with the Spirit's prompting that our attitude or action is, indeed, sin. We don't rationalize, excuse, or deny. We simply say, "Lord, you're right. I was wrong." Second, we agree that the payment of Christ is completely sufficient for our sin. We don't try to do penance to overcome the sin. We look to the cross to see the humility and weakness of Jesus, and we are humbled by his sacrifice for us . . . for me! In "Luther's Small Catechism," he instructs us, "Before God we should plead guilty of all sins, even those we are not aware of, as we do in the Lord's Prayer." And he asks some diagnostic questions to prompt reflection: "Consider your place in life according to the Ten Commandments: Are you a father, mother, son, daughter, husband, wife, or worker? Have you been disobedient, unfaithful, or lazy? Have you been hot-tempered, rude, or quarrelsome? Have you hurt someone by your words or deeds? Have you stolen, been negligent, wasted anything, or done any harm?"[7]

> **Confession, then, makes Christ's forgiveness real in our experience as we focus our hearts on the sin that grieves him and on his blood that cleanses us.**

Absolution, the forgiveness of sins, comes not from the words of our confession, but from the blood of Jesus. Paul tells us that on the cross, Christ "forgave us all our sins" (Colossians 2:13). Confession, then, makes Christ's forgiveness real in our experience as we focus our hearts on the sin that grieves him and on his blood that cleanses us. John wrote to clarify this for us: "If we confess our sins, he is faithful and just and will forgive us our sins and purify us from all unrighteousness" (1 John 1:9). Christ is "faithful" to forgive because it is his nature to fulfill his promises, and he is "just" to forgive because the price has already been paid at the cross.

True repentance consists of the realization of our sins and God's forgiveness, and it includes one more part: amendment. If we grasp in any degree the kindness of God to set us free from our guilt and sin, we will want to please him in every way possible. We won't see how close we can come to sin without sinning. We won't dabble with sinful possibilities. No, we'll stay as far away from sin as possible! We'll marvel that our Heavenly Father has forgiven us for Christ's sake, and we'll want everything we say and do to honor him.

Repentance is the normal cycle in the Christian life, not an aberrant life form! As I grow more sensitive to the Holy Spirit, I give him more opportunities to whisper to me and tell me I'm headed the wrong direction. I have choices throughout each day to pay attention to the Spirit's nudge or ignore him. I ignore him at my peril.

The order of repentance: confession, absolution, and amendment, is crucial. Too often, Christians think God demands that they change their behavior before they can go to him in confession. And some believe that they should confess first, but they think they have to change to prove to God and to themselves that they've been forgiven. Let me give you a personal illustration. I'm an active person—some would say an impetuous person—and I'm sometimes impatient when people don't move as quickly as I do. In a meeting or a conversation with an individual who isn't responding as quickly as I'd like, I can feel my anxiety rising. Those feelings have become an indicator to me that I'm caring more about my convenience than the person sitting in front of me. And that's sin. My first step is to be honest. I can tell myself, "Heck, I have every right to be upset! That guy is slowing me down!" But that blocks the cycle of repentance before it even begins. Instead, I need to say to God, "Yes, you're right. My attitude right now stinks." That's confession. Then I affirm, "Thank you, Jesus, for forgiving me for that sin. I am so grateful for it!" That's absolution. But I have another step to take. I focus on the fact that Jesus Christ died for that dear person sitting across from me, and that person is far more valuable than my convenience . . . and that changes everything.

Sometimes people ask me, "Pastor K, how are you doing?" I often answer them, "Better than I deserve." That, I believe, is an accurate response to the grace of God. Because of my sins I deserve to be cast into the deepest hell, where "the worm does not die" and "the fire never ceases," but God, in his rich mercy and love, has rescued me. Pastor and author Chuck Swindoll asked his sister Lucy which emotion she enjoyed the most. She said, "Relief." That, too, is a response to genuine grace.

Today, many church leaders focus on the glory of the resurrection, and they talk about the promise of great things God has for us. I believe that's true, but the way we get there is through the humility of Jesus Christ on Calvary's cross. Paul tells us that Christ "made himself nothing" (Philippians 2:7), and the writer to the Hebrews reminds us that Jesus "endured the cross, scorning its shame" (Hebrews 12:2). In a beautiful description of Christ's role, Paul wrote the believers in Corinth, "For you know the grace of our Lord Jesus Christ, that though he was rich, yet for your sakes he became poor, so that you through his poverty might become rich" (2 Corinthians 8:9). My theology includes both the humility of the cross and the glory of the empty tomb. One brings contrition and forgiveness; the other is an everlasting source of hope for the future.

My theology includes both the humility of the cross and the glory of the empty tomb.

Christ is awesome in power and glory, but his greatest gift to us is the pouring out of his life on the cross. In his death, we find redemption and forgiveness. One of the most amazing passages in Scripture is Paul's description of the Great Swap. He wrote, "God made [Christ] who had no sin to be sin for us, so that in him we might become the righteousness of God" (2 Corinthians 5:21). Did you get it? God took all your sins and mine, and put them on Christ at the cross where he paid for them—completely, totally, absolutely—but that's not all. In return, God has imputed to us the status of being adopted as his own children, "holy and beloved," in whom he delights. Friend, it just doesn't get any better than that!

The grace of God is incomprehensible, and it's irresistible. One of the mysteries of the faith is that we want "to grasp how wide and long and high and deep is the love of Christ, and to know this love that surpasses knowledge" (Ephesians 3:18-19). Until we see Christ face to face, we won't fully grasp the fullness of his magnificent love, but that's part of the excitement of the Christian life. The best is always yet to come, and it's incredible! We live in tension between the already and the not yet, between knowing but not knowing fully, between certainty and mystery.

God's irresistible grace presses on us like a steamroller. When it rolls over us, we are overwhelmed with gratitude, and it shapes every aspect of our lives. Like John Newton, we sing "Amazing grace, how sweet the sound, that saved a wretch like me. I once was lost but now am found; was blind but now I see." We no longer have to try to love God. We love him because we have discovered his great love for us, and we'll never be the same.

If we aren't overwhelmed by the grace of God, we will try to do "the Christian thing" to earn God's love, instead of loving and obeying out of the overflow of God's love. When we discover who we are because of God's love and forgiveness, we'll want to use the disciplines to know him better and serve him with all our strength.

GRACE AND THE SACRAMENTS

Jesus has given the church some practices we call "sacraments" to remind us of his grace and to impart his grace to us. We may be Baptist or Methodist, Lutheran or Assemblies of God, but all Christians revere the sacraments of Holy Communion and

Baptism. We may quibble (and sometimes argue vehemently) about certain aspects of these, but I want to share my own experience of the way God has used these in my own life.

The Lord himself instituted Holy Communion on the night he was betrayed. Jesus took bread and wine, gave thanks, and gave each one to his disciples. When he gave them bread, he told them, "Take and eat; this is my body," and as he passed the cup, he said, "Drink from it, all of you. This is my blood of the covenant, which is poured out for many for the forgiveness of sins" (Matthew 26:26-29). Martin Luther wrote, "These words, 'Given and shed for you for the forgiveness of sins,' show us that in the Sacrament, forgiveness of sins, life, and salvation are given us through these words. For where there is forgiveness of sins, there is also life and salvation. . . . Whoever believes these words has exactly what they say: 'forgiveness of sins.' "[8]

In the same way, Luther instructs us on the true meaning of Baptism: "Baptism is not just plain water, but it is the water included in God's command and combined with God's word. . . . It works forgiveness of sins, rescues from death and the devil, and gives eternal salvation to all who believe this, as the words and promises of God declare."[9] In both Baptism and Holy Communion, faith is essential.

When I was baptized as a child, I believe God adopted me into his family. Of course, I had no knowledge of the meaning of the event at the time, just as I had no conscious awareness of the day of my birth. Each provided an environment for me in which to grow. Baptism "saved me," that is, it put me in a condition of grace in which God could work powerfully and specifically in my life to lead me to grow in my faith in him (Titus 3:4-7). In infant baptism, my parents and god-parents made a promise to God, but more importantly, God made a promise to me. He said, "You are my own." I believe that people who are baptized as adults also receive a promise from God, even as they make a promise to him.

GRACE AND THE DISCIPLINES

I'm afraid that too often, the word *grace* has come to mean something passive, stagnant, and theoretical. But a grasp of our desperate need and God's incomparable gift energizes like nothing else in the universe! As we turn now to the seven doors of spiritual growth, we need to remember that grace removes blockages in our relationship with God and compels us to love him, serve him, and obey him with all our hearts.

The message of redemption is that we were hopeless and helpless sinners, but God loved us so much that Christ paid the ultimate sacrifice for us. The disciplines of the faith, then, aren't rigid measuring rods to see if we measure up to God's harsh standards. No, indeed! They are open doors with God inviting each of us to come to him, to experience his love and be challenged by his purpose to change the world one life at a time. Jesus is behind each door of the disciplines, inviting us to use them to know him better.

> **They are open doors with God inviting each of us to come to him, to experience his love and be challenged by his purpose to change the world one life at a time.**

I want to close this chapter by asking you two questions about relating to God by grace. The first question is this: How sure are you that if you died today, you'd go to heaven to be with God? The second question is closely related to this. Imagine standing before God and he asks you, "Why should I let you into heaven?" What would you tell him?

I hope you now know the answer to the second question. It's not by our works, our goodness, or anything else we do to try to earn God's favor. I'd answer the question: "God, I sure don't deserve to be in heaven because I'm certainly not good enough, but I've trusted in Jesus' death on the cross for me." I'm convinced God would invite me in and say, "Welcome home."

You may be just beginning to learn about Jesus, or you may have been to church all your life. If you aren't sure your sins are forgiven by the grace of God, I want to give you an opportunity to express your desire to God. The exact words aren't the important thing. You can use your own, or you can use these:

"Lord Jesus, I desperately need your grace. My sins have separated me from you, and I need to be forgiven. Thank you for dying on the cross for me. Right now, I want to affirm that you have forgiven me, you love me, and you've given me eternal life. Help me to grasp your grace so that more and more, my life reflects your goodness and greatness. Amen."

Our confidence in our relationship with God doesn't come from fleeting feelings; it comes from the promises of God to forgive us, to adopt us into his family, and to give us his Spirit to comfort, correct, and guide us. If you've just trusted in Christ, tell somebody about it as soon as you can. Your friends would like to know!

I live with an enormous sense of gratitude for all God has done for me. All Christians have their own stories of God's great grace, and I'm always amazed that God would reach down into the darkness of my heart to turn on the lights of his love and forgiveness. I can look at all the physical blessings God has given Elaine and me, and I'm so thankful, but these gifts don't compare to the richness of our family life. And beyond even that incredible gift is the amazing fact that I, who deserved nothing, received the incomparable wealth of forgiveness and life from the hand of Almighty God. And it's all because of his grace.

Martin Luther wrote, "I believe God made me and all that exists. He has given me my eyes and ears, my reason and senses. He has given me a house and home, fields, cattle and all my goods. He guards and protects me from all evil. All this he grants purely out of Fatherly divine goodness and mercy, without any merit or worthiness in me. He has redeemed me, a lost and condemned person. He has purchased me, not with gold or silver, but with the holy and precious blood of his innocent Son. All this, that I may be his own." [10] This insight is the source of my deepest joy, thankfulness, relief, and peace. I hope it's the same for you!

THINK ABOUT IT

1. Why are wonder and mystery important in grasping the grace of God? What is so wondrous and mysterious about grace?

2. What are some evidences of treating God like he is "a specially attentive waiter"? How do you think that makes God feel? How can that attitude be changed?

3. Read Galatians 3:15-25. What is the purpose of the law? Describe how it leads people to Christ (verse 24).

4. Review the section, "The Riches of Grace," which describes grace as "God's Riches at Christ's Expense." Which of the five insights about grace means most to you? Explain your answer.

GOING DEEPER

1. Review the three types of self-righteousness. How can so many people in the church have these attitudes? Describe how they short-circuit our experience of God's grace.

2. Describe your role and the Holy Spirit's role in the three elements of repentance: confession, absolution, and amendment.

3. Describe a time when you were most convinced of the grace of God. How did God communicate his grace to you at that time? What differences did it make in your relationship with him, your attitude, your purpose, and your actions?

2. Witness

THE DOOR OF OPPORTUNITY

"But you are a chosen people, a royal priesthood, a holy nation, a people belonging to God, that you may declare the praises of him who called you out of darkness into his wonderful light" (1 Peter 2:9).

"Do what you are." —Os Guinness

Verb or noun? It makes a difference. When we think of the word *witness,* do we envision *the act* of telling others about Christ, or do we think of *the person* who serves as a witness? Peter claimed, "We were eyewitnesses of [Christ's] majesty" (2 Peter 1:16), and that fact shaped every attitude and action for the rest of his life. We need to understand that we are nouns before we act as verbs.

I was talking to a friend about this book, and as I described the flow of the chapters a slight smile crossed his face as he asked, "John, most authors know that evangelism is pretty threatening to people, so they put it last in their books. But you . . . What are you thinking?" (That was a nice way of saying, "John, you're nuts!" But he's much too polite to say something like that.)

I told him, "Everything we do, everything we say, and everywhere we go springs from our sense of identity. *Who we are* determines *what we do.* Yes, I know people are uncomfortable with evangelism, but I'm talking about something far bigger, far more important than a behavior. Our identity is absolutely central in our grasp of the Christian life. We are witnesses whether we understand it or not, whether we proclaim the message of Jesus often or seldom, and whether we speak that message with our lives or our words.

IDENTITY

In his thoughtful and challenging book, *The Call,* author and cultural critic Os Guinness goes to the root issue of the Christian life. His definition of *calling* is "the truth that God calls us to himself so decisively that everything we are, everything we do, and everything we have is invested with a special devotion and dynamism lived out as a response to his summons and service."[11]

We are called first to someone, then to something—we are called to Christ before we serve in his cause. The biblical authors grasped this truth in dramatic and powerful ways. In the Old Testament, from the patriarchs to the prophets, God reminds them again and again, "I will be your God, and you will be my people." Their most fundamental concept of identity was their relationship with God. And in the New Testament, John tells us the astounding fact (only diminished because we're so familiar with the phrase) that we are "children of God" (John 1, 1 John 4, etc.). Remember, we were enemies of God, hopeless and helpless sinners, but God, in his great grace, has "chosen, adopted, forgiven, and sealed" us (Ephesians 1). Paul instructs us to flee from sin because sin doesn't belong in our lives. Our bodies are "temples of the Holy Spirit," and we are no longer our own, because we have been bought with the price of Christ's blood (1 Corinthians 6:18-20). These are marvelous statements about our identity!

> **We are called first to someone, then to something—we are called to Christ before we serve in his cause.**

In a powerful statement to people who had been cast out of their homes by persecution, Peter reminds them of their true identity, not as unwanted wanderers, but as members of God's royal family. He wrote, "But you are a chosen people, a royal priesthood, a holy nation, a people belonging to God, that you may declare the praises of him who called you out of darkness into his wonderful light" (1 Peter 2:9).

Witnessing, then, isn't reserved for people from certain denominations that give tracts to people on street corners or hold tent crusades. It's not primarily a verb, an act we perform (or choose not to perform). Instead, it's an expression of our new, basic, consuming identity as beloved children of the King. It flows from the core of our being, not tacked on the outside from time to time.

I'm including this discipline first because all the others flow from a proper understanding of it. And the source of our identity is the grace of God. In *The Purpose Driven Life,* Rick Warren famously began, "It's not about you." He's exactly right. The Christian life is initiated by God and sustained by God. As we grasp our identity as his chosen, beloved children, we will want to please him. We'll be comforted by his grace and challenged by his incredible purpose to change lives. Don't miss this. It's the most important lesson we can ever learn.

THE DISTORTION

Os Guinness observes that many Christians fail to live out their calling because they have dichotomized the sacred and the secular. They compartmentalize their lives: They devote Sunday morning, and perhaps Bible study or prayer from time to time, to Christ, but during the rest of the week, they hardly give God a passing thought. On a larger scale, many believe that people in full-time church work are doing God's will, but the rest of us are second-class citizens in the kingdom of heaven. Both of these dichotomies, of time and of vocation, are false and destructive. They rob us of the joy of seeing God work in every aspect of our lives, at home, at work, in the neighborhood, and at church—not just at church. And they prevent us from seeing our roles, no matter how mundane, as vital to God's purposes in the world.

Martin Luther wrote, "The works of monks and priests, however holy and arduous they be, do not differ one whit in the sight of God from the works of the rustic laborer in the field or the woman going about her household tasks, but that all works are measured before God by faith alone. . . . Indeed, the menial housework of a manservant or maidservant is often more acceptable to God than all the fasting and other works of a monk or priest, because the monk or priest lacks faith."

In a more earthy reflection, Luther commented, "The mother who is wiping the dirty butt of a baby is giving a witness of Christ just as much as a priest who is consecrating the elements." When we respond to Christ's invitation to come to him, all of us—pastors and plumbers, missionaries and mothers—become his servants. There is no pecking order of value or dichotomy of roles.

> When we respond to Christ's invitation to come to him, all of us—pastors and plumbers, missionaries and mothers—become his servants.

In his letter to the Colossians, Paul gave instructions to "get rid" of selfishness and "clothe yourselves" in the character of Christ. He then outlined a number of specific behaviors and attitudes that come from a proper understanding of our identity in Christ. At the end of that list, he concluded by saying, "And whatever you do, whether in word or deed, do it all in the name of the Lord Jesus, giving thanks to God the Father through him." No dichotomy of time: whatever you do. And no dichotomy of vocations: all of us. And every moment of every day is devoted to "the name of the Lord Jesus." In that culture, names signified character. Paul is saying, "Live every moment of your life to reflect the grace, forgiveness, love, purpose, and strength of the one who gave his life for you." That's our calling!

THEY'RE WATCHING

People are watching us to see if our commitment to Christ makes any difference in how we live. We are witnesses "on the stand" all day, every day in front of a jury of our spouse, children, neighbors, friends, and co-workers. What do they see?

I'm convinced that most people aren't looking for perfection. They're looking for honesty, integrity, and authenticity. They want to see if our actions match our words, and some of the most powerful words we can ever say, to those closest to us as well as casual acquaintances, are these three little words: "I was wrong." If we communicate that we are never wrong and we have to be in complete control at all times, people may be amazed at first, but soon they see beneath the façade.

Trying to convince others we're perfect is a defense against them finding out the ugly reality that we are fallen, needy people. But to keep up this farce, we have to lie to others, and maybe to ourselves as well. Sooner or later, though, the hard exterior shell of perfection cracks. In those crushing moments, we realize that our lies have isolated us from God and a few people who love us. That's a steep price to pay for a phony façade.

Ken Blanchard wrote one of the best-selling business books of all time, *The One-Minute Manager.* Several years after its publication, I heard Ken speak at a conference, and he said that if he could make one change in his book, he would include the point that a healthy office atmosphere would be greatly enhanced if managers would invite people to confess their faults to one another and forgive each other. If that's important in an office, it's crucial in the home.

The message of the grace of God in Jesus Christ is the most hopeful one in the world. It promises hope, joy, and purpose far beyond anything we have ever known. But a conversion experience does not eradicate our sinful natures. In his most famous treatise on the Christian life, Paul described our forgiveness in Christ in great detail, but he lamented, "I do not understand what I do. For what I want to do I do not do, but what I hate I do"

(Romans 7:15). Some have tried to say that Paul was referring to a time before he was a Christian, but he is writing in the present tense. Others claim that he must have been "carnal" at that point in his life, but it's incomprehensible that Paul could be writing perhaps the most powerful account of the faith the world has ever known, the book of Romans, while he was not walking with God. No, I believe Paul is giving an honest account of the tension we all sense in our walks with Christ. We know his love, but we groan because we long for more. Our ambition is to please him, but we are easily tempted to live for the approval of people. We are created for eternity, but we live as if today is all that matters. Yes, we are "new creations," but that new creation is a decidedly mixed bag until our transformation is complete when we meet Jesus the moment after we take our last breath. Our fallen natures aren't eradicated when we become believers, but we are no longer "under obligation" to them to obey them. We now have a choice.

Our ambition is to please him, but we are easily tempted to live for the approval of people.

Our response to those choices determines our credibility in the eyes of those who watch us. They don't expect to see perfection, but they long to see consistency. Our spouse, our children, our friends, and everyone around us longs to sense Christ's character being formed in us. We can start where we are. We can stop playing games to try to fool people, and we can be honest about the process of growth. Honesty is a risk. There's no question about it. And certainly, we have to be wise about who we tell and how much we tell, but when I've taken the risk to be honest with people, the vast majority of them have extended more grace than I could imagine. In these precious and powerful moments, we learn to trust each other more deeply than ever before, and we build love and respect that are the lifeblood of relationships.

I certainly have a dark side in my life. Because I'm a pastor, people sometimes put me on a pedestal, but the truth is that I struggle with the same temptations that every other man experiences. If I claim to be above it all, I lose credibility with people, and my lie blocks my relationship with God. Being honest about the darkness in my heart, though, surfaces my needs and is the springboard to a deeper experience of God's great grace and richer relationships.

I remember a message I preached about the reality of darkness in our lives and how God can use it to deepen our dependence on him. After the message, I walked over to a good friend and told him, "Gary, I need you to pray for me. I'm really struggling with some things in my dark side."

Gary looked at me and said, "I can tell you are, but you need to know that I love you no matter what's going on in your life. You can count on me." And he gave me a big hug.

I can't tell you what his words and the look in his eyes meant to me that day. His embrace was a manifestation of the grace of God. I needed to be reassured that God's goodness was greater than the mess in my life, and Gary was there for me. True friendships are formed in the crucible of trouble when people don't run away or criticize when a friend shares a struggle.

I believe that Paul was well aware of the darkness in his heart to the day he died. He had been a leader of the Jews, and he had captured, persecuted, and murdered Christians. But God's grace found him. After his conversion, he continued to call himself "the chief of sinners" (1 Timothy 1:15). But his awareness of his sinful nature didn't haunt him. He didn't wallow in guilt and shame. Instead, it sharpened his understanding of God's love and forgiveness, and it amazed him for the rest of his life. As we read Paul's letters, over and over again he breaks out into praise of God for his marvelous grace. In the same way, the awareness of our sinful nature need not haunt us. It can rivet our hearts on God's great love for us.

Being authentic requires us to distinguish between guilt and shame. Guilt is the message that "I did something bad," while shame is the crushing message that "I am a bad person." Shame kills, but guilt is the door to forgiveness. Our identity in Christ, that we are beloved children of our Heavenly Father, helps us distinguish between the Holy Spirit's tap on our shoulders that an attitude or action is sin, and the destructive, demonic lie that because we have sinned, God has turned his back on us.

Listen to the Holy Spirit's whisper, but fight against Satan's accusations that you are scum because you've sinned too badly or too often. Paul recognized the power of these lies when he wrote, "We demolish arguments and every pretension that sets itself up against the knowledge of God, and we take captive every thought to make it obedient to Christ" (2 Corinthians 10:5). The "arguments" and "pretensions" are those thoughts that rumble around in our minds that we can never do enough to overcome a particular sin, or that God's patience has run out, or that we can't feel good about ourselves if a particular person is angry or disappointed in us, or that if people knew what was really in our hearts they'd leave us. Paul instructs us to lay these lies at the feet of Christ, see what his word says about these things, and find hope and peace again in his forgiveness and truth. And again, we focus on our identity in Christ and bask in his kindness, affection, and good purposes for us.

> **Listen to the Holy Spirit's whisper, but fight against Satan's accusations that you are scum because you've sinned too badly or too often.**

When we think we can be perfect and sinless, we *idealize* who we think we should be and then *idolize* ourselves. But we can never live up to those lofty—and unbiblical—expectations. We either become arrogant because we find someone who is not as good as we are, or we beat ourselves up because it seems that everybody else is better than we are. Pride or shame, those are the two options in perfectionism. Grace, in contrast, allows us to be honest about God's love as well as our sinful natures. We are, as theologians would say, *simul lustus et peccator,* simultaneously just and sinful, a double image. In observing people for many years, I've seen that those who embrace the reality of both grace and their sinful natures are the ones who live the most thankful, authentic Christian lives and earnestly seek to follow Jesus Christ.

Some of the nicest and most meaningful compliments I've ever received are from people who have said, "Pastor, thank you for being real. I can identify so much with the struggle you shared, and I appreciate the hope that you've given me that God is with me through it."

In those moments, I tell them, "Thank you so much. You may not know it, but the first sermon I preach each week is to me because I need to hear it so much." The grace of God makes me the most optimistic, enthusiastic person in the world. Being honest about my sinful nature reveals my desperate need for God's love and forgiveness, humbles me, and keeps me dependent on him. Does this sound a bit schizophrenic? Maybe, but it's the reality of living in the tension of the Christian life.

ALL OF ME, FOR HIM

Another false dichotomy focuses on the nature and source of our talents. This misunderstanding confuses many Christians and deadens their zeal because they devote some of their talents to God but reserve others for themselves. For example, the emphasis on spiritual gifts is very helpful to millions of Christians, but some believe that they are honoring God only when they use their talents in the local church. They fail to see that all of their talents and abilities come from the hand of God and are to be used in every sphere of life.

All of our efforts can be devoted to God so that we represent him effectively. When we grasp the fact that every talent we possess is a gift from God, we become thankful for his grace, and we stop comparing ourselves to others. This insight shatters pride.

A missionary talked graphically yet humbly about how God had used him to lead a tribe in Indonesia to Christ. At one point, he remarked, "Every ability I have is a gift from God, and it is my privilege and responsibility to receive them gladly and use them. I don't boast in my talents. They are gifts, and a person would never boast of a gift." He quoted Paul's insight in his letter to the Corinthians, "For who makes you different from anyone else? What do you have that you did not receive? And if you did receive it, why do you boast as though you did not?" (1 Corinthians 4:7)

As chosen, adopted, loved, and gifted children of God, we discover our true calling by trying a number of ministries to see which ones God blesses, and we enjoy a sense of fulfillment. Our task isn't to find a single perfect place to serve, but to sharpen our abilities and follow God's leading. Guinness writes, "The truth is not that God is finding us a place for our gifts but that God has created us and our gifts for a place of his choosing—and we will only be ourselves when we are finally there."[12]

Many Christians, I fear, aren't "themselves" because they haven't yet tapped into the vast reservoir of God's grace. They are still trying to earn enough points by being better than someone else or following enough rules. Grace frees us from this bondage and compels us to love God with all our hearts and enjoy our status as beloved children. Only then will we long to please him instead of pleasing ourselves, and only then will we be on the path of becoming fully devoted followers of Christ.

PRESENTING . . . THE AMBASSADOR

The more we are overwhelmed by the grace of God, the more we'll want to represent him every moment of every day, in every endeavor of our lives. And we'll want our purposes to line up with his purposes. We are first and foremost witnesses (noun) before we witness (verb) to others about the message of Jesus. I trust I've made that point, and now I want to turn to the amazing truth that God has chosen to use you and me in his great cause: "to seek and to save the lost."

In his second letter to the believers in Corinth, Paul says that God "gave us the ministry of reconciliation: that God was reconciling the world to himself in Christ, not counting men's sins against them. And he committed to us the message of reconciliation" (2 Corinthians 5:18-19). God could have used angels or monkeys or skywriters, but instead, he gave the ministry and the message of reconciliation to you and me. "We are therefore," Paul continues, "Christ's ambassadors, as though God were making his appeal through us. We implore you on Christ's behalf: Be reconciled to God" (verse 20).

> **God could have used angels or monkeys or skywriters, but instead, he gave the ministry and the message of reconciliation to you and me.**

In these few verses, we find an extension of our identity, a clear statement of cause, and the motivating passion of the heart. Ambassadors represent the interests of their government to a foreign land. You and I represent the King of Kings and Lord of Lords on earth as citizens of the kingdom of God. Our cause is his cause: to help people grasp the grace of God so they can escape condemnation and bridge the gap between themselves and God. Reconciliation occurs when enemies become friends. It is the restoration of a relationship that was meant to be rich, warm, and wonderful, but was shattered by betrayal. Our attitude in communicating this message of grace isn't distant and detached. It's passionate and kind. We "implore" or beg people. Does that sound odd, maybe even offensive? It's not, if we recognize what's at stake—all of eternity—for those who hear our message.

Most people become Christians when someone they know, a family member or friend, lives an authentic Christian life and communicates the message of reconciliation. In most cases, it takes both a person as a *model* and a clearly articulated *message* for people to "get it." We have focused most of our attention in this chapter on our identity in Christ because his character must be formed in us if we are to be good models for others. But it's an incredible thrill to communicate the message and let people respond. I want to share a few stories with you about some thrills God has given me.

God can use us even when we're timid and barely have enough faith to open our mouths.

I answered God's call to serve him in a small mission church in Irving, Texas, in 1970. I was told that my job was to grow the church by leading people to Christ, and I have to tell you, that scared me to death. I grew up as a good German Lutheran, and we don't do things like that! I'd never been taught to tell people how to trust in Christ as their Savior, but I knew God wanted me to meet people where they lived and introduce them to myself, and then to Jesus. I went from house to house knocking on doors, and I prayed that nobody would be home. (How's that for great faith?) Surprisingly, the first people to answer the doorbell invited me to come in. I told them as best I could about the grace of God, and the whole family trusted in Jesus! In fact, their children were the first people I baptized at that church.

The goal of evangelism is to impart life, not cram a message down someone's throat.

A dear lady who was attending the church in Irving lived right across the street, but her husband Tom wouldn't come with her. I met him and invited him to come to the church, but he immediately shook his head and told me, "No, I don't want anything to do with religion."

I asked if we could just get together and talk. We met several Saturday mornings and talked about all kinds of things. After a while, Tom began to trust me, and he confided that he had studied for the ministry years ago, then he told me, "Pastor, I was overwhelmed by all the rules and regulations. I felt totally inadequate to keep going, so I abandoned the whole thing. That's why I don't go to church any more."

Tom and I continued to meet, and he was open to me sharing about the wonderful grace of God. A couple of weeks into our discussions about God's grace, he turned to me and smiled, "Pastor, this is just too good to be true!" He trusted in Christ and became one of the most outstanding lay leaders in that congregation.

People are searching for truth. Just because they've looked in the wrong place doesn't mean they won't be open to the gospel.

Charlie is a man in our church who has a wonderful ministry with young people. He teaches guitar, and he's involved in our music ministry. Not long ago, Charlie's friend, Jason, was invited by our recreation coordinator to offer a tai chi exercise class at the church. A lady in the church came to see me a couple of weeks later to ask some questions. She said she had attended the class and was surprised that it didn't include prayer or any mention of Jesus. "But I was given these two booklets," she announced as she placed them on my desk. One was a book of exercise movements, but the other described the philosophy of tai chi, combining influences from Confucius, Buddha, and Jesus. "Pastor," she told me, "you may want to check into this a bit more."

I knew Charlie's heart for young people, so I asked him to tell me more about Jason and his classes. Charlie smiled and said, "Yeah, Pastor, I've been working on him! I've been telling him about Jesus." We talked about my concerns for the class, and Charlie understood the problem very well. His solution wasn't to condemn Jason, but to ratchet up his communication of the gospel.

Not long after our meeting, Charlie called to tell me, "Jason just accepted Christ in my office, and he wants to meet with you." We met regularly as Jason devoured the Word of God. What a thrill it was several weeks later when I was privileged to baptize

Jason in the Christian faith. At the time of his baptism, he gave a powerful personal testimony of how God was transforming his life.

God's grace transcends all barriers of race, nationality, age, or religion.

My brother Melvin helped found the International School in Hong Kong in the 1950s. In 1996, he invited me to go with him on a trip to Mainland China. We couldn't afford it at the time. We had two children at Baylor University and another in law school, so finances were pretty tight. I was completely surprised when members of our church gave me a nice gift of cash for my 25th anniversary at Gloria Dei, and Elaine told me to use it to go with my brother to China. I called Melvin and we planned our trip. Several other family members and friends joined us.

Before I got on the plane in Houston, I prayed, "Lord, please give me an opportunity to lead someone to Jesus." A wonderful, young Chinese lady who worked for the Chinese government's International Tour Service met us in Shanghai as our national tour guide. For convenience, she told us to call her Laurie. I asked Melvin if it would be appropriate for me to talk to her about Christ. He nodded and suggested that I be sensitive to her culture and her role as our guide. For the next couple of days, I talked to Laurie to get to know her. I sat next to her on a flight from Beijing to Xian, and I asked, "I'm curious, are you a Christian?"

She replied, "No."

I asked another question: "Are you a Buddhist?"

Laurie shook her head, "No, I'm not."

"Then," I asked, "how would you describe yourself?"

She looked at me and said, "I'm a seeker."

I smiled and said, "That's great. Do you know much about Jesus?"

She shook her head, so I asked her, "Would you allow me to tell you about him when we have some time on this trip?"

Laurie nodded, and a few days later at a beautiful spot in

Guilan, China, my cousin, John, spotted a church steeple in the distance. We walked to it and found they were having a church service the next evening, a Saturday. Melvin and I asked the group if they'd like to attend. They said, "Yes!" About two-thirds of our group went with us, including Laurie.

That night, the church was having a special "seeker service" with a traveling evangelist speaking, of course, in Chinese. One of the most remarkable and beautiful moments of the whole trip occurred when we sang "Amazing Grace." The local people sang in their language, and we Americans sang in ours. After the service, Laurie talked to the evangelist for a few minutes. As we walked back to our hotel, I asked her if she'd like to talk more with us about Jesus.

For the next couple of hours, we walked Laurie through the biblical narrative about Jesus. After a while, I asked her, "Does this make any sense to you? If so, where do you see yourself on this spiritual journey?"

She thought for a moment and replied, "I think I'm on the way."

I told her, "In the New Testament is a book called Acts. In it, those who followed Jesus were called 'people of the way.' I think you're becoming one of them."

Two years later, Laurie's path intersected with Melvin's again. She had come to trust in Christ as her Savior, and Melvin baptized her. She became a very devout and vibrant believer, and when I met her on a return trip to China four years later, she told our group how she had become a Christian. There wasn't a dry eye in the room. She repeated her story five years later for another group I led to China. She shared that the night before she was baptized she had experienced an excruciating spiritual struggle. The devil filled her mind with doubts. She wondered if the only reason she was going to be baptized and follow Jesus was to identify with Americans or to please Melvin, but she fought through her fears and doubts to realize that she was being baptized because she truly believed Jesus was the Savior—her Savior.

As Melvin and I have talked about this remarkable experience he has reminded me, "John, salvation is always a miracle. You and I could never have pulled this off, but God's spirit worked faith in Laurie's heart."

God initiates and produces faith in each one who believes.

We talk about "making a decision to trust Christ," or "accepting Jesus," and from man's perspective, that's true. But in the unseen world, God is the initiator, and he uses all kinds of things to draw people to himself. I enjoyed the wonderful benefits of a loving home. My parents taught and modeled the love and strength of God, so when I learned that God is my Father, it wasn't much of a leap for me to believe.

> **John, salvation is always a miracle. You and I could never have pulled this off, but God's spirit worked faith in Laurie's heart.**

Others, though, have come to Christ on more difficult roads. I received an email from a man in our church who told me about a business partner whose wife recently died at the age of 35, leaving him with two small children. God spoke to this bereaved father in a dream. His wife appeared to him and pulled his face close to hers and told him, "All the Jesus stuff we talked about. It's all true." This certainly isn't the usual way that God speaks to the broken hearts of lost people to assure them of his presence and forgiveness, but God, I'm convinced, will use almost any method to get his message across.

EVERY OPPORTUNITY

I love the story in Acts 26 when Paul stood in front of King Agrippa to give an account of his faith in Jesus. Paul was a little Jewish man who had been a prisoner for a while. The guards led him into a marbled hall with dignitaries dressed in beautiful robes. Agrippa asked Paul to speak, and he told the king the story of his persecution of Christians and the day Jesus appeared to him on the road to Damascus. Paul explained that on that day, Jesus told him, "Now get up and stand on your feet. I have appeared to you and appointed you as a servant and as a witness of what you have seen of me and what I will show you. I will rescue you from your own people and from the Gentiles. I am sending you to them to open their eyes and turn them from darkness to light, and from the power of Satan to God, so that they may receive forgiveness of sins and a place among those who are sanctified by faith in me" (Acts 26:15-18).

Then Paul looked at the king and told him, "So then, King Agrippa, I was not disobedient to the vision from heaven." That is my hope and prayer, too. On the day I meet Jesus face to face, I want to be able to say to him, "Jesus, I was not disobedient to the vision from heaven."

When Festus, the governor, heard Paul's story, he interrupted and accused the little man of being insane! In my life, too, there are those who think my faith in Jesus is a little nuts, but my trust in God is a Spirit-given response to the deity and humility of Jesus Christ.

Agrippa was familiar with the claims of Christ. He must have sighed deeply when he said to Paul, "Do you think that in such a short time you can persuade me to be a Christian?"

I would have loved to see the look on Paul's face when he answered, "King, I don't care if it's a short time or a long time, just so you—and all those here today—will respond to Jesus."

You and I have the unspeakable privilege of using our words and actions to represent Jesus to those around us. Most of us won't have the opportunity to represent him to kings and governors, but people around us—those we love and all those who are loved by God—are watching us all day, every day.

At the end of his letter to the Colossians, Paul asked them for prayer. He wrote, "And pray for us, too, that God may open a door for our message, so that we may proclaim the mystery of Christ, for which I am in chains. Pray that I may proclaim it clearly, as I should" (Colossians 4:3-4). By that time in his life, Paul could have said, "Hey, I've done enough for God. I've traveled all over the known world, been beaten and whipped, and suffered in every imaginable way. I deserve a break!" But he didn't have that attitude at all. Instead, even in jail, he asked his friends to pray that God would open a door of opportunity for him to share the message of the cross. And he, the one who wrote so many of the New Testament letters, asked them pray that his message would be clear. He was humble and dependent, and God used him to "turn the world upside down."

SOME SUGGESTIONS

Our identity as children of God, redeemed sinners, and ambassadors for Christ is the foundation for our choices to represent him. Let me offer a few suggestions to help you absorb these truths:

- Affirm and clarify your identity in Christ. Examine the passages of Scripture in this chapter, read through Paul's letters and look for other powerful statements of your identity in Christ, and examine passages from the Old Testament that add depth to your understanding of your identity in Christ. Memorize some of the verses to burn those truths into your mind and heart.

- Ask God, "Search me, O God, and know my heart; test me and know my anxious thoughts. See if there is any offensive way in me, and lead me in the way everlasting" (Psalm 139:23-24). Then listen for the prompting of the Holy Spirit to reveal anything that needs to be confessed and forgiven.

- Create reminders that every activity of every day, no matter how hidden or mundane, is an opportunity to represent Christ. Write Colossians 3:17 on your computer, put a pebble in your pocket, or find some other way to remind you to devote every minute of every day to Christ. You'll forget from time to time, but that's not a big deal. Just start over and try to do the next thing in the name of Jesus. Sooner or later, you'll develop the habit.

* Reflect on God's redemptive purpose in the world "to seek and to save the lost," and align your purposes with his. Think about both the privilege and the responsibility of being his ambassador.

* Be intentional about imparting the message of the gospel. Have neighbors over for dinner, invite people to church, give books about Jesus, share your testimony of how God awakened faith in you, and invite people to affirm God's grace for them.

* Regularly pray for two or three people who don't know Christ.

Paul's passion—his consuming, driving zeal—was for Christ and his love for the lost. Growing churches (and growing Christians) find a way to share their faith with people who are lost and dying without the Savior. If our efforts come from legalism's "got to's," we'll soon quit. But if our zeal is fired by the incomparable grace of God, which we've experienced in the forgiveness of our own sins, we, like Paul, will look for every opportunity to tell people about Jesus.

> But if our zeal is fired by the incomparable grace of God, which we've experienced in the forgiveness of our own sins, we, like Paul, will look for every opportunity to tell people about Jesus.

THINK ABOUT IT

1. Before you read this chapter, did you think of "witness" as a verb or a noun? How do you think about it now? Explain your answer.

2. Review Os Guinness's definition of calling: "the truth that God calls us to himself so decisively that everything we are, everything we do, and everything we have is invested with a special devotion and dynamism lived out as a response to his summons and service." In what ways does this reflect a sense of identity instead of just behavior? In what ways does this identity result in behavior?

3. Read 1 Peter 2:9-10. How do you think these words might have struck people in Peter's day who read them when they were outcasts, wandering because they were being persecuted for their faith? What do these verses mean to you?

4. What are some specific ways you can be a more effective ambassador for Christ?

GOING DEEPER

1. Reflect on Colossians 3:17 and Martin Luther's quote: "The works of monks and priests, however holy and arduous they be, do not differ one whit in the sight of God from the works of the rustic laborer in the field or the woman going about her household tasks, but that all works are measured before God by faith alone." How would it change your life if you saw each moment as an opportunity to do everything you do "in the name of Jesus"?

2. Think about the section on shame and reflect on 2 Corinthians 10:3-5. What are some ways you can fight more effectively against thoughts filled with shame?

3. Take some time to apply (or plan to apply) the suggestions at the end of the chapter. Which ones seem most helpful to you? Explain your answer.

3. Worship

THE DOOR OF WONDER

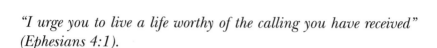

"I urge you to live a life worthy of the calling you have received"
(Ephesians 4:1).

"When we see Jesus for who he really is, we savor him. That is, we delight in him as true and beautiful and satisfying.... Christ is most glorified in us when we are most satisfied in him. And when we are satisfied, we are crucified to the world." —John Piper

I often hear people ask one another, "How did you like worship Sunday morning?" or "Wasn't our worship beautiful? I love those hymns!"

Yes, I certainly hope people worshipped God during the church service and during the singing, but worship is far bigger than an hour—or the singing during that hour—on Sunday mornings. The depth and breadth of our worship is a direct result of our sense of identity. If we've divided our lives into two separate boxes, the sacred and the secular, then we only worship during those times we've deemed sacred. During the rest of our week—in fact, the vast majority of it—we may not even think about God at all.

Our word *worship* is an abbreviated form of the old English word "worthship." It is, in its essence, devotion to someone or something. We can worship our cars, a sports team, fashion, a person, or God. But Jesus said we really cannot have two objects of worship. He told us, "No one can serve two masters. Either he will hate the one and love the other, or he will be devoted to one

69

and despise the other" (Matthew 6:24). There is only one throne in our hearts, and we choose who sits there.

Paul told the Ephesians to "live a life worthy of the calling you have received" (Ephesians 4:1). When are we to live in a way that pleases God? All day, every day. In what circumstances? All of them. In which relationships? With every person. Worship is an awareness and adoration of the grace of God in the details of our lives. When we relegate worship to brief intervals, we miss the joy of seeing God at work in our everyday life, decisions, and relationships.

In my early 20s, I was a teacher, principal, and youth director in a small church and school in Havertown, Pennsylvania. One Sunday afternoon, I invited the youth group at my church, about a dozen high school students, to join me in the backyard for a Bible study. These kids really wanted to study the Scriptures, and I asked them, "Great. What do you want to study?"

A couple of them responded, "Let's talk about worship."

We looked at some passages, and I explained to them that worship isn't an act—it's a lifestyle. I told them worship starts with God's initiative and is stimulated when God expresses himself to us through his word. He created us to reflect his image, and that can happen 24 hours a day, seven days a week. They asked questions about various activities to see if they qualified under the banner of "worship," and I explained, "If you aren't doing something *apart* from God's will, then *anything* and *everything* you do is worship."

At that moment, a girl named Gaye leaned back, took a deep breath and asked, "Mr. Kieschnick, does that mean that when I rolled up my hair this morning when I was getting ready for church, it was an act of worship?"

I almost laughed as I told her, "You bet it was!"

She had always thought worship was confined to church attendance, but now she realized her whole life—Sunday and Tuesday, morning and night, private and public times—could be devoted to God. I've always remembered the look on Gaye's face that afternoon and how that insight changed her life.

WORSHIP BEGINS WITH THE REVELATION OF GOD

Worship, a life of devotion, is our reasonable response to God's gracious initiative. It begins with God revealing himself to us. One of my favorite passages in the Bible is Isaiah's account of his vision of God's glory. He recorded, "I saw the Lord seated on a throne, high and exalted, and the train of his robe filled the temple" (Isaiah 6:1). Angelic seraphs flew around the throne, and they called out praise: "Holy, holy, holy is the Lord Almighty; the whole earth is full of his glory." The prophet tells us: "At the sound of their voices the door posts and thresholds shook and the temple was filled with smoke." What an awesome scene!

This wasn't a figment of Isaiah's imagination or a Hollywood film full of special effects. This was an encounter with the living God. Isaiah was minding his own business that day, but God showed up! In the revelation of his glory, God first overwhelmed Isaiah with his sinfulness and his need for grace, and when the prophet responded in confession and repentance, God gave him a clear, compelling purpose.

> **Isaiah was minding his own business that day, but God showed up!**

It's the same way with me—not as dramatic, of course, but the principles are exactly the same. God shows up to me every day in his word. In the pages of Scripture, I see who God is and what God is like. The words aren't just ink on paper. The Bible is God's divine message to me to reveal himself, overwhelm me with his grace, and give me a purpose I would never pursue and could never accomplish on my own. Revelation isn't something that can be crammed into an hour a week. The holiness and majesty of Almighty God consumes my entire life . . . if I'll let it.

Helmut Thielecke wrote about the transforming power of God's revelation to us. He asked, "What was there before you were born? What was there the day of your baptism? What was there when you were on your mother's knee? What was there when you were confirmed? What was there when you went to school and later when you got married? What was there when you saw the birth of your own children? What is there at the day of your death, and what is there on the other side? It is the word of God."

God's word is "near to us." We simply need Jesus to make some clay and apply it to our blind eyes to make us see. When that happens, our hearts will overflow with praise and thanks, and we'll want every attitude and action to reflect the grace and power of God. We are "the people of his pasture." In worship, I become fully aware of who God is, all he has done to make me his redeemed child, and his incredible purposes for my life.

Three truths from God's word help us "live a life worthy" of our calling: realizing that we are God's *possession,* recognizing God's *presence,* and embracing God's *purpose* for us.

WE ARE GOD'S POSSESSION

Many times in his letters, Paul calls himself and us "bond-servants." That term may not mean much to people who enjoy freedom in a democracy, but it meant a lot to readers in the first century. Paul's term reminds us of an agreement between masters and slaves many years ago. Just after Moses listed the Ten Commandments, he gave instructions for godly living in his culture. In that day, if a person owed money but couldn't repay the debt, he became an indentured servant. After he had worked several years to pay off his debt, he was set free. But if his master had been unusually kind, the servant could choose to stay. We read, "But if the servant declares, 'I love my master and my wife and children and do not want to go free,' then his master must take him before the judges. He shall take him to the door or the doorpost and pierce his ear with an awl. Then he will be his servant for life" (Exodus 21:5-6).

From that moment, people would see the hole in the man's ear and know he had chosen to remain a bondservant because he had experienced his master's love. This is a wonderful picture of our response to God's grace in our lives. Our debt has been paid, and we are free to do whatever we want, but because we love our master, we choose to stay to serve and honor him.

The bondservant recognized that the master had the responsibility to provide for him and protect him, but the master also had the right to give directions and expect obedience. It was love, though, that formed the bond between master and servant. Love changed everything.

> **Our debt has been paid, and we are free to do whatever we want, but because we love our master, we choose to stay to serve and honor him.**

Jesus told us, "I will never leave you; never will I forsake you" (Hebrews 13:5). In response to his gracious promise, we can tell him, "Lord, I belong to you." Years ago, a pastor recommended that we carry that insight into every circumstance we encounter. When God gives us wonderful encouragement, we can rejoice and say, "Lord, I belong to you, and I realize you are the one who gave me this gift. Thank you so much!"

When we are lonely, we can pour our hearts out to God and say, "Lord, I belong to you, and I know you are with me right now."

When we are filled with self-pity, envy, or jealousy because life doesn't seem fair, we can pray, "Lord, I belong to you, and you have the right to determine my circumstances."

And when we face difficulties and excruciating decisions, we can tell him, "Lord, I belong to you, and I know you will lead me and use this situation to make me more dependent on you, no matter how it turns out."[13]

Worship, then, takes root in our acknowledgement: "You are not your own; you were bought at a price. Therefore, honor God with your body" (1 Corinthians 6:19-20). This realization provides both relief and accountability; we are relieved at the thought that a loving, wonderful, gracious God cares for us, yet we also realize he owns us and deserves every ounce of devotion we can muster.

WE LIVE IN GOD'S PRESENCE

King David was described as "a man after God's own heart." He was passionate about God's glory, and he deeply appreciated God's forgiveness of his sins. David lived with the constant recognition that he was in the presence of God, all day, every day. In one of his most beautiful psalms, David begins and ends by acknowledging that God's eyes "search me" and "know me." This isn't a fleeting or casual grasp of our condition. God knows every single detail about us: every action, every thought, every desire, and every molecule of our being. Since he lives in eternity, God knows what we are going to do or say before they occur.

The penetrating presence of God can be—and in fact, should be—disconcerting. If we see God as a kind but slightly senile grandfather, we will believe we can get away with almost anything. If we see him as a vending machine, we'll use him when it's convenient for us and forget about him the rest of the time. But if he is the all-knowing, all-seeing, ever-present God of the universe, our feelings about his presence might be a bit, shall we say, mixed!

David, in fact, wanted to run and hide. He wrote,
"Where can I go from your Spirit?
　　Where can I flee from your presence?
If I go up to the heavens, you are there;
　　if I make my bed in the depths, you are there.
If I rise on the wings of the dawn,
　　if I settle on the far side of the sea,
even there your hand will guide me,
　　your right hand will hold me" (Psalm 139:7-10).

What does it mean to live with an awareness of the presence of God? It means we, like the bondservant, realize that our master knows everything about us, and his gaze never leaves us for an instant. We are assured of his constant care, and we realize that every decision makes a difference. Every thought, word, and deed brings honor or dishonor to the one who paid the incalculable price to rescue us from death and darkness. This isn't "feel good" theology, but it's an accurate understanding of the nature of God and our rela-

> **This understanding produces both affection and awe, and both are essential in living a life of true worship.**

tionship to him. This understanding produces both affection and awe, and both are essential in living a life of true worship.

We may or may not sense God's presence. In fact, when we are most desperate for it, God may withhold it to deepen our faith. Author Henri Nouwen wrote with great insight that we can trust God even when we don't sense he is there, and during those times, we realize how desperately we need God. In times of darkness, we can still be confident of God's loving presence. Nouwen wrote, "Our life is full of brokenness—broken relationships, broken promises, broken expectations. How can we live with that brokenness without becoming bitter and resentful except by returning again and again to God's faithful presence in our lives?"

Is God watching when you sing hymns at church? Of course, but he's watching just as intently when you are driving down the street, when your eyes wander too long on a magazine ad, when you lend help to a friend, when you lose heart and complain because things didn't go your way, when you trust God in the middle of a dark time for your family, and at every other moment of every day. The more we realize that we live under the watchful eye of Almighty God, we will respond with respect, obedience, and affection.

WE EMBRACE GOD'S PURPOSE FOR US

Today, many people think of "ambition" as a selfish, negative trait, but ambition itself is neutral. It is right or wrong depending on the focus of the person's desires. Paul used this word to describe our zeal for God: "Therefore also, we have as our ambition, whether at home or absent, to be pleasing to [Christ]" (2 Corinthians 5:9 NASB). I watch people as they talk about the Astros, the Texans, their college football team, or the local high school team, and I see genuine passion! Their eyes widen, their voices become more intense, and they lean forward as they talk about their hopes and dreams for their team. Many of these people invest a lot of money and time to watch these teams play. That's what Paul was talking about when he said our ambition is to please Christ. The value of his grace and his cause is so immense that our hearts race and we gladly sacrifice everything to pursue them.

Paul said that you and I were created for a purpose. On the broadest level, that purpose is to honor God, but each of us has been given a specific role to fulfill. Paul told the believers at Ephesus, "For we are God's workmanship, created in Christ Jesus to do good works, which God prepared in advance for us to do" (Ephesians 2:10). Paul had just explained that their entrance into a relationship with God was by his grace, and now, as an extension of that grace, God has made us partners with him to accomplish his purposes on earth. And his purposes are far bigger than an hour on Sunday morning!

Worship, then, isn't just praise and thanksgiving. It's far bigger than that. Worship is a life that is devoted to pleasing God every moment of every day. Throughout the Scriptures, we find clear insights and directions to help us live in a way that is worthy of the one who bought us and watches us. I want to highlight just a few:

God's purposes at home

First, we realize that our families are gifts from the Lord. (Sometimes, we'd like to give them back, but that's another story!)

The psalmist said that "children are a gift from the Lord," and in Genesis, we read that God gave Eve to Adam in marriage. We are to honor our parents, and in fact, this command is the first one with a specific promise. If we see them as gifts from God, he will cause our lives to prosper (Ephesians 6:1-3).

The home is the greenhouse for God's word to be modeled and nurtured. This environment is so important that God speaks often and powerfully about these relationships. Husbands are to love their wives. How? "Just as Christ loved the church and gave himself up for her" (Ephesians 5:25). Women, I have a hunch that you would be pretty thrilled if your husbands gladly sacrificed their own goals and desires for your sake, all day, every day. And men, if we love our wives this way, I think their response will make us pretty happy!

In a home that is focused on God's nature and purposes, every moment is an opportunity to teach and model biblical truth. Disciplining children changes from trying to control them to imparting God's principles to them, and we avoid the extremes of being too harsh or too lenient.

> In a home that is focused on God's nature and purposes, every moment is an opportunity to teach and model biblical truth.

A family filled with the grace of God changes lives—those in the family and all those who watch them. Not long ago, a lady listened to some friends talk about their families. One described children wrecking their lives on drugs and a husband emotionally distant. Another had experienced similar problems in the past, but she and her husband had turned to Christ a few years ago. In those years, God had restored their marriage and their relationship with their kids. Reflecting on these conversations, the lady remarked, "This may sound obvious, but it really does make a difference when a family follows God's principles."

You might be saying, "Wait a minute, Pastor K. Aren't you drifting a long way from the idea of worship?"

Thanks for asking. The answer is, "No, not at all." Worship is an attitude, a longing to please God, all day, every day. We do that when we're alone or in a meeting, at home or in the office, in the den or in the bedroom, at the game or in church. Our attentions and affections express our worship of something or someone all the time. I'm only encouraging us to choose to worship God everywhere we go.

God's purposes at work or at school

One of the biggest problems in the lives of believers today is that few see their careers connected to God in any meaningful way. Their lives are segmented into the sacred and the secular, and school and work are decidedly in the secular camp. In these endeavors, they don't seek God's guidance, they don't look for God to work, and they don't bathe these activities in prayer and the word of God.

Work and school are also gifts from God. Yes, part of the Fall described in Genesis is that we have to work "by the sweat of our brow" to earn a living, but before sin, God gave Adam work to do in the Garden. Meaningful work is a gift from the Father, and he allows us to see the fruit of our labor. God has given us abilities and opportunities to provide for our families, but under the guidance and authority of Christ, the goal isn't to make enough money so we can provide every luxury we can imagine. God wants us to follow his leading in our vocations so that our work itself reflects the goodness and greatness of God. How can that happen?

> God wants us to follow his leading in our vocations so that our work itself reflects the goodness and greatness of God.

First, we need to trust God to direct us in our educational pursuits and careers. Many factors contribute to our decision to pick one career over another, but God needs to be in the center of the mix. Most people are exactly where God wants them to be. They function in their strengths, and they contribute to the common good. The vast majority of them, however, have never contemplated that their goal, their ambition, is to please God at work, which is worship. I asked a man what difference it would make if he saw his work as a place where he could honor God. He replied with wide eyes, "It would change everything! In every conversation I have, I'd think about what God wants to accomplish. And in every choice I make for the company, I'd consider the ethical standards that are consistent with the character of God." He's exactly right.

Some men and women, though, are pursuing the wrong careers. Maybe they've been pushed into a major in college or a job at a company because their parents wanted them to pursue those things, or maybe they just drifted without a purpose and eventually landed at a place they could work. No career pursuit is fulfilling all the time, but the way we spend our time and energies needs to have some sense of rightness, a blend of comfort because we do it well and challenge to do even better. If we don't experience this powerful blend of comfort and challenge, at least for a long period, we should ask God if he has other plans for us.

In the past decade or two, a lot of Christian organizations have targeted the workplace as a ministry opportunity. I applaud these efforts. Most of them help people experience God's presence and purpose on the job, train people to apply biblical principles such as ethics and conflict resolution, and shape people's values so they learn to align their purposes with God's.

Over the years, I've had the privilege of watching quite a number of men and women worship God through their work. In many of these cases, they came to a realization (I'm convinced God took the initiative to show them) that every aspect of their lives was under the authority and care of God. Work is no different. They began to see their hours at work as opportunities to please God, and by the grace of God, they experienced inner conflict when they saw their companies exhibit unethical business practices. These men and women stood up for honesty, resolved conflict with other employees, and worked hard to be examples for others. And whenever they had the chance, they graciously and appropriately told people about Jesus.

I was explaining this perspective to some people not long ago, and a woman shook her head and said, "Pastor K, that's great, but you don't know my boss. He's a bear. He doesn't give a flip about biblical principles, resolving conflict, or anything that God cares about."

From the tone of her voice and the look on her face, I could tell that this lady suffered under this man's leadership. "You have three options," I replied. "You can keep struggling under your boss, playing his games, and driving yourself crazy. Or you can quit and find another job. (And actually, that might be a good option in some cases.) Or you can have the attitude of a slave."

She smiled and said, "OK, I'll bite. What do you mean 'the attitude of a slave'?"

I turned in my Bible to Colossians, and I read a few verses to her. "Remember," I told her, "this is about slaves, not just employees. These folks had no choice, but you do. Listen to this." I read, "Slaves, obey your earthly masters in everything; and do it, not only when their eye is on you and to win their favor, but with sincerity of heart and reverence for the Lord. Whatever you do, work at it with all your heart, as working for the Lord, not for men, since you know that you will receive an inheritance from the Lord as a reward. It is the Lord Christ you are serving. Anyone who does wrong will be repaid for his wrong, and there is no favoritism" (Colossians 3:22-25).

"You see," I explained, "you aren't just serving your boss at work every day. You are serving Jesus Christ. You don't have to play games with him. You can serve him with honor and integrity, speaking the truth without fear. And you can be sure that some day, you will be richly rewarded by God for your good attitude, your faith in him, and your hard work."

The Scriptures say a lot about careers and money. The Proverbs, Ecclesiastes, the Sermon on the Mount, and a host of other passages explain God's perspective about the meaning of our careers. In those passages, we find many good motives for honoring God at school and work: to use the talents God has given us, to experience fulfillment, to let our light shine there so that people find out more about Christ from us, to provide for our families, and to make God smile. In school and at work, our efforts are for his honor, so we follow the highest standards of integrity. In all of these motivations, we worship as we express our devotion to God.

God's purposes in the community

We represent God and demonstrate our devotion to him in every encounter in our neighborhoods. Chats with neighbors, shopping at the grocery store, driving down the street, and a hundred other activities put us in contact with people Christ died for. They aren't just warm bodies; they are lost or redeemed souls.

One of the best ways to demonstrate our affection for Christ is to care for "the least of these" in our communities. Jesus said that a measure of our devotion to him is our help for those who are hungry, thirsty, lonely, naked, sick, and in prison (Matthew 25:34-40). You may not have many naked people in your neighborhood, but many of those who survive hurricanes, fires, or tornadoes have little more than the clothes on their backs. In our community, "the least of these" are single moms, the elderly,

> **One of the best ways to demonstrate our affection for Christ is to care for "the least of these" in our communities.**

widows, those who have experienced a death in the family, and others like them. Worship isn't just a pleasant feeling about God. We worship when we see needs and take action to meet them in the name of Christ. And people notice.

Jesus came "to seek and to save the lost," and those people are all around us. Paul asked people to pray for God to open doors for him to share the gospel with lost people. You and I need to ask God for wisdom about how we can be lights in our communities, too. He'll show us. He always does.

God's purposes at church

Finally, we're back at church! I believe worship on Sunday mornings can be a highlight of the week, not because one day or one hour is more sacred than the others, but because the family of God gathers to express its heart of love for him. Our task is to focus our hearts completely on Christ during that time.

Before you come to church, prepare your heart. If you know which passage of Scripture will be taught that morning, read it and ask God to speak to your heart. Pray for an open heart, and pray for each person and each aspect of the service. If God shows you that you have unresolved conflict, respond, repent, and take steps to resolve it. Like every couple, sometimes Elaine and I have come to church with something wrong between us. Peter advised husbands to "be considerate" of our wives and "treat them with respect . . . as heirs with you of the gracious gift of life, so that nothing will hinder your prayers" (1 Peter 3:7). I sure don't want my prayers to be hindered, so I need to clear up anything with Elaine before we walk through the doors on Sunday morning. (And of course, that principle applies every day of the week, not just Sunday.)

Pray for specific people who need God's touch that morning, and expect God to work in people's lives. Our pastoral staff prepares for worship each week by praying with some dedicated "Pastor's Prayer Partners" in the church. Some Sundays, I'm emotionally or physically exhausted, and I don't have any idea how I can preach God's word with power and clarity. On a few occasions when these people have laid their hands on me and prayed, I've actually felt the warmth of God's Spirit. Every Sunday, I ask God for a unique sense of His presence for each of us who lead and each person who comes to our church.

Come to church with a sense of expectancy, anticipating that the God who has called you by his grace will answer your prayers. Caedmon's Call is a contemporary band out of Houston. A line in their song, "Carry Your Love," expresses my heart's desire. They sing to God, "Send down your word. We are eager to hear it."[14] My prayer for myself and every person who joins us is that we will be eager to hear God's word and quick to respond to him in faith.

When you walk in the door of the church, go through the process of clearing out all distracting thoughts. Put those people and situations in God's hands, and focus your heart on God, the music, the message, and the people around you so you can be fully present. Some Sundays, I have to confess to God several times during the service that my mind is drifting—and I'm the pastor! If that happens to you, don't interpret it as a flaw in your character. Just refocus your mind on God. When you sing, think about the

> **Some Sundays, I have to confess to God several times during the service that my mind is drifting—and I'm the pastor!**

message of the songs, and express them in praise to God. When you hear the message, ask God to give you a responsive heart. When you greet people, realize that each one may carry a heavy burden or have a joy to celebrate. Take a moment to share the load or the joy.

One of the most meaningful moments for me during the service is at the altar of Holy Communion. At those times, God's presence is richly personal and powerful. The post-Communion prayer explains the meaning of the event: "May this salutary meal increase my faith in you, God, and my love for my brothers and sisters." The Lord's Table, then, manifests the true and real presence of Christ in the company of God's people. It is a constant reminder, drawn from Hebrew culture, of using a past reality to foster a present experience. And our experience of the elements at the Table foreshadows the Lamb's feast we'll enjoy in heaven. Sometimes I ask our congregation, "Is this the last time we'll enjoy this meal on this side of eternity? Maybe our next meal together will be in heaven's banquet hall."

And as you leave the church service, don't focus on the silly hat some lady wore, the sleepy choir member, or the relative merits of this illustration or that point in the sermon. Initiate conversation at lunch about the ways you can apply the principles taught from the Scriptures, and encourage each person who is taking even the smallest step of faith.

RENEWAL

Worship is an all-the-time thing requiring all of me. If I hesitate to offer every fiber of my being, I simply don't grasp my identity in Christ. Paul wrote to the Romans, "Therefore, I urge you, brothers, in view of God's mercy, to offer your bodies as living sacrifices, holy and pleasing to God—this is your spiritual act of worship. Do not conform any longer to the pattern of this world, but be transformed by the renewing of your mind. Then you will be able to test and approve what God's will is—his good, pleasing and perfect will" (Romans 12:1-2).

Notice that Paul makes this statement in chapter 12 after he had described the grace, mercy, forgiveness, and saving plan of God for 11 chapters. With that unshakable foundation of the grace of God, he "urges" believers to respond in faith. This is not a bland suggestion. He pleads with us like a father or mother pleads with a child to make good choices for his own good.

But our choice is not to become a dead sacrifice, but a living one. As we interact with people and respond to problems and opportunities at home, at school or work, in our communities, and at church, we worship God by pursuing his purposes and living in a way that is worthy of him. Each morning, we can get up and say, "Good morning, God!" instead of growling, "Good God, it's morning." God offered himself to us in the body of Jesus Christ, and we offer our bodies—all that we are and all that we have—back to him as living sacrifices. Paul describes this sacrifice as "holy," which means set apart for God's purposes, "pleasing to God," because the Spirit of God is alive in us and is working through us, and a "spiritual [or reasonable] act of worship," which implies that devoting our whole lives to God makes perfect sense in light of God's mercies.

As we have seen in earlier chapters, though, we still have an active, evil nature that tempts us to pursue selfish things. For that reason, Paul couples the call to active worship with the admonition to confess, renew, and repent. We recognize the thoughts that deceive us, and we acknowledge those thoughts to God. Nature, though, abhors a vacuum, so we don't just kick out the wrong thoughts. We have to replace them with thoughts that are holy, pure, right, and helpful—thoughts that come from God's word. Then, and only then, can we test our minds and our actions against God's standard so that we can stay riveted on God's "good, pleasing, and perfect will."

When we talk about "God's will," some people get all hung up on analyzing everything they do to make sure it's God's will. I tell them, "Relax. If the Scriptures don't forbid it, enjoy it. If it's wrong, the Holy Spirit or another believer will tell you." I agree with Augustine when he said, "Love God with all your heart and do as you please." That's powerful and sound advice.

For my mind to be renewed, I have to be still. I'm an activist. I love to get up and get going, and it's extremely difficult for me to sit alone and still so I can focus my mind and heart on God's word and God's will. But in those times of stillness, I can hear the whisper of the Spirit, and I cherish those moments when I sense that God is speaking to me. Most often, he reminds me of a

> **Most often, he reminds me of a passage of Scripture that reveals his way and his will in a situation, and sometimes his Spirit nudges me in a direction I hadn't anticipated, and I sense his peace.**

passage of Scripture that reveals his way and his will in a situation, and sometimes his Spirit nudges me in a direction I hadn't anticipated, and I sense his peace.

The renewal of our minds is a lifelong process. As we grow in our relationship with Christ and learn more of his word, we'll see patterns in our lives and notice where we usually trip up. Then we can avoid those things. We'll also see where God uses us most effectively, and we'll pursue those activities. As we grow, we'll increasingly depend on God in every circumstance in our lives.

Growing in our faith, though, doesn't mean we become perfect in this life. In some ways, spiritual growth means that we become more aware of our desperate need for God's grace. God said, "Be perfect because I am perfect." Some people say, "See, we can be perfect now," but others tell us, "Well, Jesus didn't really mean that at all. It's impossible." Jesus meant every word. Perfection is his standard, with no exceptions and no qualifications. But there's no possible way we can achieve his perfect standard of holiness, and that's why we must throw ourselves on the mercy and grace of God. Jesus is perfect now, but our perfection will come after we die and meet Jesus face to face. For now, we increasingly realize our crying need for the grace of God, and we are satisfied that God meets that need. Paradoxically, being ruthlessly honest about our sins sets us free. Only in being honest do we expose our need for grace, and God's grace always brings forgiveness, relief, hope, and peace.

The Scriptures tell us that an entire unseen universe exists, one in which the forces of darkness and the force of light war against each other. If I don't get away to reflect on the things of God and ask him for insight and direction, I react only to the visible things in my world. But I desperately need to see beyond the visible into the supernatural realm, where God's purposes are more real than the things I can see with my eyes. To be honest, I am most attentive to the unseen world when I'm in trouble. But I'm not alone. Paul described a host of problems and threats in his second letter to the Corinthians, and he told them, "Therefore, we do not lose heart. . . . For our light and momentary troubles are achieving for us an eternal glory that far outweighs them all. So we fix our eyes not on what is seen, but on what is unseen. For what is seen is temporary, but what is unseen is eternal" (2 Corinthians 4:16-18).

BARRIERS

Let's be honest. We live in a real world with genuine struggles. It is estimated that 25 percent of Americans experience clinical depression at some point in their lives. A recent survey of Ivy League students shows that 17% of them have used self-mutilation (cutting or burning) to relieve internal pain. Some 50 million Americans struggle with an addiction to drugs, alcohol, gambling, sex, or food, and each of these adversely affects at least two others who are trying to cope in a family full of anger and lies. Divorce is rampant in our culture, and bitterness rears its ugly head in intimate and casual relationships. The statistics for the church are, in most respects, no different from the general population. All of these facts show us plainly that we "have sinned and fall short of the glory of God."

God isn't a genie in a bottle that we call to come out and fix things from time to time, and he hasn't given us any quick, easy formulas for a happy and successful life. The message of the Scriptures is that God has given us doors of opportunity, but each opportunity contains its own challenge. The lusts of the flesh, the charms of the world, and the deception of the enemy of our souls threaten us at every step. We need to identify the barriers to a lifestyle of devotion to God. I want to target just a few:

- Lack of compassion—When we are under pressure, one of the first qualities to slip away is genuine care for people in pain, even those in our own families. Instead of caring for them, we begin to resent their needs because they get in our way.

- Short tempers—Stress heightens our expectations of people and causes us to snap at them when they don't perform up to our standards. Lofty and unrealistic expectations inevitably lead to demands, not grace, and conflict, not understanding.

> **Lofty and unrealistic expectations inevitably lead to demands, not grace, and conflict, not understanding.**

- The fog of despair— Sooner or later, unfulfilled expectations result in despair and a loss of hope and joy. Things that used to bring us joy now bore us, and we can't even seem to think clearly anymore.

- Psychosomatic illnesses—Physicians estimate that 70% of their patients' complaints are a direct result of stress. Common symptoms include chronic headaches, gastro-intestinal problems, and muscle pains. When we are under intense stress, adrenaline levels escalate. Sleep patterns are interrupted, and people either can't sleep, or they sleep too much.

- Isolation— Loneliness and thoughts of despair cause people to withdraw from others, even those who genuinely care for them. Isolation, though, only compounds the problem because it provides fertile soil for more discouraging thoughts of self-pity.

- On edge—Too much stress causes many of us to shut down, but other people develop a heightened awareness to everyone and everything. They try to "read" people and situations so they can respond quickly to control them or avoid them.

- Fantasies—Excessive stress creates a desire to escape. We daydream about getting away from the causes of stress and finding relief and excitement. In their milder forms, these fantasies are completely harmless, but they are paths to destruction if they lead us to adultery, stealing, cheating, or any other behavior that is apart from God's plan.

- Anger at God—Stress can easily become a normal part of life. In fact, many of us don't think twice about all the stress we experience. At this point, we can't imagine life without it. But sooner or later, our resentments build, and minor irritations fester into major conflict. Our expectations rise, and anger mounts. This anger, though, often centers on those in authority: our boss, spouse, parents, and God. Some of us won't let ourselves express anger at God, but the psalmists had no such inhibitions. They were painfully honest about their deep disappointment that God failed to bail them out and that he took so long to show up when they were in need.

In his article, "Diagnosing Hurry Sickness" in *Leadership* magazine, author and pastor John Ortberg identified two common signs of stress: speeding up and multi-tasking:

- "Speeding up. You are haunted by the fear that you don't have enough time to do what needs to be done. You try to read faster, lead board meetings more efficiently, write sermons on the fly, and when counseling, you nod more often to encourage the counselee to accelerate."

- "Multiple-tasking. You find yourself doing or thinking more than one thing at a time. The car is a favorite place for this. Hurry-sick [people] may drive, eat, drink coffee, listen to tapes, shave or apply make-up, direct business on the car phone—all at the same time."[15]

- Burnout—When people experience excessive stress over a long period, they inevitably suffer a devastating meltdown.

An article, "Burnout: Signs, Symptoms, and Prevention" vividly describes the causes and symptoms:

"Burnout produces feelings of hopelessness, powerlessness, cynicism, resentment and failure—as well as stagnation and reduced productivity. These stress reactions can result in levels of depression or unhappiness that eventually threaten your job, your relationships and your health.

Burnout is associated with situations in which a person feels: overworked, underappreciated, confused about expectations and priorities, concerned about job security, overcommitted with responsibilities, and/or resentful about duties that are not commensurate with pay.

Burnout can occur when you feel you are unable to meet constant demands, and you become increasingly overwhelmed and depleted of energy. Debilitating sadness, anger or indifference can set in. You begin to lose the interest or motivation that led you to take on a certain role in the first place."[15]

A wrong diagnosis of the problem leads to wrong solutions, creating even more stress. Many of us who suffer under excess stress conclude that we need to work just a little harder to get more done. We put in more hours at work, and we drink a lot of caffeine to stay alert. When we feel out of control, we become more demanding. All of these efforts only compound the problem, and our stress level escalates even more. At some point, we need a shot of objectivity from a trusted friend or the tap of God's Spirit to remind us of God's purposes for us. Without that blast of spiritual reality, we continue to suffer the consequences of the stress treadmill.

> **At some point, we need a shot of objectivity from a trusted friend or the tap of God's Spirit to remind us of God's purposes for us.**

GRACE AND WORSHIP

Worship begins with the revelation of God. God sustains it as we respond to his grace in every aspect of our lives, and it continues through good times and bad because we trust that God's purposes far surpass our own selfish desires. A heart devoted to God doesn't guarantee a smooth life—Jesus' experience certainly proves that point. But genuine devotion clarifies our direction and purifies our motives. The young German pastor, Dietrich Bonhoeffer, committed himself to honoring Christ, and in the 1930s and 40s, he took an unpopular stand against Hitler and his Nazi regime. During World War II, Bonhoeffer was imprisoned for speaking out against Nazi oppression. Alone in prison and facing a future of torture and death, Bonhoeffer never regretted his commitment to Christ. He wrote: "I am sure of God's hand and guidance. . . . You must never doubt that I am thankful and glad to go the way which I am being led. My past life is abundantly full of God's mercy, and, above all sin, stands the forgiving love of the Crucified."[16]

Just days before the Allied army could free him, the Nazis executed Bonhoeffer. He went to the gallows with a clear mind and a full heart. His faith and dignity impressed his fellow prisoners and even the guards. Bonhoeffer's reward for a life of faithfulness, obedience, integrity, and eventually a martyr's death was God's affirmation of his faithfulness. During his imprisonment and until the end of his life, he sensed the presence and purpose of God. His life and his death were demonstrations of worship.

For most of us, a life of worship isn't nearly as dramatic as Bonhoeffer's, but it's still thrilling to see God use us to change lives. The more we are convinced that we are God's possession, not our own, that we live each moment in the presence of the almighty God, and that he has entrusted us with a sacred purpose, our lives will increasingly reflect his nature and his cause. The older I get, the more I have a sense of wonder at the mystery of God's infinite goodness and greatness. Every moment is an adventure of following Christ, and continual worship is the door of wonder at the goodness and greatness of God. We constantly experience his presence and purpose, and we need to remove all the barriers we can identify. That's what it means to be transformed more into the image of Jesus. That's what worship is all about.

THINK ABOUT IT

1. Before you read this chapter, how would you have defined "worship"? How would you define it now?

2. Read Ephesians 4:1 and Isaiah 6:1-9. How do these passages connect? How did the revelation of God move Isaiah to want to live a life worthy of his calling?

3. Describe how each of these biblical principles shape our concept of worship:

   —We are God's possession.

   —We live in God's presence.

   —God has given us a purpose to fulfill.

4. From the concepts in this chapter, what is one specific thing you will do differently:

   —at home?

—at work or school?

—in your community?

—at church?

GOING DEEPER

1. What are some reasons it is difficult for many of us to fully realize we are God's possession, we live in God's presence, and God has a purpose for us in every sphere of our lives? What can we do about those reasons (or at least one or two of them)?

2. What are the best tools and techniques you've found to renew your mind so that you think God's thoughts and fulfill his purposes?

3. Review the barriers to a life of worship. In what ways does stress affect your motivation and capacity to experience a lifestyle of worship?

4·Connections

THE DOOR OF ENCOURAGEMENT

"And we urge you, brothers, warn those who are idle, encourage the timid, help the weak, be patient with everyone" (1 Thessalonians 5:14).

"One of the highest of human duties is the duty of encouragement. . . . It is easy to laugh at men's ideals; it is easy to pour cold water on their enthusiasm; it is easy to discourage others. The world is full of discouragers. We have a Christian duty to encourage one another. Many a time a word of praise or thanks or appreciation or cheer has kept a man on his feet. Blessed is the man who speaks such a word." —William Barclay

Sometimes I tell people at our church, "Some of you may not like me, but that's too bad. As a matter of fact, I don't like some of you. But that's beside the point. We're brothers and sisters in Christ, and we're going to be together for eternity, so we'd better learn to get along and love one another!"

God made us for relationships—with him and with each other. In the Garden, Adam was in the perfect environment and without sin, but "it was not good for man to be alone." It's the same in our fallen world today. It's not good for any of us to be alone. When we read the New Testament, we find a host of "one another" passages. We are to "love one another," "encourage one another," "exhort one another," and "forgive one another." Believers are to be so interconnected that we are called "the body of Christ." This wonderful term implies that we respond to the head, Jesus Christ, and that every bone, muscle, ligament, organ, and blood cell is vitally important for the body to function with grace and strength.

Ney Bailey is a traveling speaker for Campus Crusade for Christ. She has worked with thousands of men and women over the years. She has seen the growth and freedom that comes from encouragement, and she's seen the devastation resulting from harsh treatment. She observed simply, "People live for encouragement, but they die without it." The fact is, we are hurt most deeply in relationships, and we are healed most completely in relationships. They mean everything to us.

Years ago, during a difficult time in the church's life, Elaine and I felt really stressed. For some strange reason, we chose that time to build a new house, so our stresses compounded. We sold our house and moved into an apartment while the new house was being built. With all the stresses at work and at home, we were really strung out. During that time, my brother Melvin called. He said he was traveling to Houston, and he asked if he could stay with us for a few days. When I told Elaine, she responded, "This apartment is so small we can't have anybody stay with us!"

But I said, "We'll find some room."

She looked at me and said bluntly, "Do you see any extra beds for him to sleep on? We just don't have any room!"

"We'll find a place for him," I told her. "He's my brother."

Later, Elaine told me, "When you said, 'He's my brother,' I knew I had to change my mind and invite him to come, and I'm so glad we did."

Melvin came to our little apartment to spend a few days with us, and during that time, God used him in incredible ways in our lives. He listened intently as we poured out our frustrations and hurts, and he pointed us to Christ time after time. When we had difficulty seeing God's hand at work, he saw it. When we couldn't find a way to trust God with our situation, he affirmed God's goodness and sovereignty. At the end of his time with us, Melvin wrote a beautiful letter to confirm that God had something wonderful in store for us, but he acknowledged that God's path is sometimes a difficult road. At that crucial point in our lives, Melvin's love and wisdom meant the world to Elaine and me.

That's the kind of encouragement we can give to one another. It transforms lives. Letting someone into our lives might be inconvenient, but the results can be wonderful.

> **At that crucial point in our lives, Melvin's love and wisdom meant the world to Elaine and me.**

PLAYING GAMES

At the core of many people is a deep, but often hidden, sense of fear. Our fear is often compounded by hurt and anger. This trilogy shapes our responses, raises our defenses, and causes us to play games in relationships. We feel compelled to *please* people, *prove* ourselves, and *hide*. These games, we're convinced, will help us gain a sense of value and avoid more hurt.

Some of us are driven to please people. We read the expressions on their faces so we can change our behavior to suit them. If a powerful person has an opinion, we're eager to go along. If a hurting person has a need, we jump in to meet it. Every behavior is designed to cause other people to appreciate us, but we're like puppets on a string, dancing every time they tug with praise or criticism.

Others are driven to prove themselves. They may have been criticized or ignored before, but never again! They are competitive—no, more than that: They see every conversation as a win-lose affair, and they are determined to win. They may use intimidation, knowledge, or some other form of power to be one-up on those around them. Those who have to prove themselves wake up every day wondering if they will meet someone more intimidating, more knowledgeable, or more powerful in some way.

Still others have given up on pleasing people to win approval, and they lack the confidence to intimidate. They just hide. Their goal in life is to give in or get away to avoid conflict. If someone asks their opinion, they say, "Oh, I don't care. Whatever you want is fine." People who hide can almost vanish in a crowded room.

Under stress, people who please, prove, or hide simply become more intense about playing their game. *Pleasers* worry even more about people's opinions of them, *provers* become even more demanding, and *hiders* evaporate into the woodwork more completely.

We tend to associate with people who make us feel good and who don't threaten us. Years ago, I heard an insightful message about the Prodigal Son. As you recall, he left home with his inheritance and blew it all on "loose living." Do you think he was by himself out there? No way. He was partying with his buddies. They loved him as long as he was buying drinks and paying for the games, but when his money ran out, so did his "friends." The young man found himself destitute and alone. In Jesus' story, he said, "No one would give him anything to eat."

Pleasers gravitate to needy people they can fix and powerful people who will tell them what to do. Provers gather weaker people who are easily intimidated by their power. And hiders only hang out with people who make virtually no demands on them.

Is this a picture of the body of Christ? Not at all.

AUTHENTICITY

The key to healthy relationships isn't controlling people, and it isn't perfection—it's authenticity. We don't have to be sinless and completely loving. Nobody expects that (at least, no reasonable person expects that), but people expect us to be genuine, honest, and sincere. The goal, then, isn't to play the game so well that we win approval, dominate people, or avoid any conceivable chance of conflict. The goal is to love and be loved, to develop strong relationships based on earned trust, and to care for people with "non-possessive warmth," a love that doesn't have to control.

The mission statement of our church is: "To reach out and help people experience a growing relationship with Jesus Christ and his church." Because of sin, people are alienated from God, from other people, and from the best God has for them. The grace of God operates in relationships just as it does in individual hearts. In his letter to the Ephesians, Paul described the hatred and distrust between Jews and Gentiles, and he said that both groups find forgiveness in the cross. Then he wrote, "For [Christ] himself is our peace, who has made the two one and had destroyed the barrier, the dividing wall of hostility. . . . His purpose was to create in himself one new man out of the two, thus making peace, and in this one body to reconcile both of them to God through the cross" (Ephesians 2:14-16).

> The goal is to love and be loved, to develop strong relationships based on earned trust, and to care for people with "non-possessive warmth," a love that doesn't have to control.

God didn't create some of us to live and work alone and the rest of us to be in community. All of us are part of his body. All of us are essential for the church to function properly. That doesn't mean that we all have the same functions, and it doesn't mean that we all think exactly the same way. "Iron sharpens iron" and sparks fly, but that's the way "one man sharpens another."

In the same passage, Paul tells us that all believers (yes, Lutherans and Baptists . . . and every other denomination!) are citizens of the same kingdom, members of the same household, and parts of the same building. He wrote: "Consequently, you are no longer foreigners and aliens, but fellow citizens with God's people and members of God's household, built on the foundation of the apostles and prophets, with Christ Jesus himself as the chief cornerstone. In him the whole building is joined together and rises to become a holy temple in the Lord. And in him you too are being built together to become a dwelling in which God lives by his Spirit" (Ephesians 2:19-22).

As citizens of God's kingdom, we share the same privileges and responsibilities. God rules over us, and we follow his directions to serve in his kingdom. We may have different roles, but we are all proud ambassadors, and we are all humble servants. As members of God's household, we are an extended family. I love the fact that believers in Ghana, Indonesia, Bolivia, and the other far reaches of the earth are my brothers and sisters in Christ. We may get to choose our friends, but we can't pick our family members. Our Father does that for us. We don't have to agree on everything, and we don't even have to like each other. But in the family of God, we are called to love each other just as Jesus loves us (1 John 4:11), forgive one another just as Jesus forgave us (Colossians 3:13), and accept each other just as Jesus accepted us into his family (Romans 15:7).

Paul also describes the church as a building, with the apostles as the foundation and Christ the cornerstone. Each of us is a brick or a board, dry wall or plaster, a light fixture or plumbing in the construction of this beautiful temple. We need each other to complete the building, and we stand or fall as one. In fact, we are indispensable to each other, but we don't just make things up as we go along. Our stability is based on the teaching of the apostles and the grace and truth of Christ himself.

When you take a casual glance around your church's sanctuary, what do you see? In most churches, you'll find some people who are a lot like you, but you'll also find people you'd never choose as friends. We have different backgrounds, ethnicities, abilities, roles, and passions, but we all belong to Jesus Christ. We are citizens of his kingdom, members of his family, and interconnected materials in his building.

THE REAL MCCOY

The concept of the church as a family isn't sterile and lifeless. It's rich and real, and people value these relationships so much that they change the direction of their lives to enjoy them more. I know a number of people who have turned down promotions that would have sent them to other communities because they wanted to stay connected to our church. I'm sure every church that loves Jesus can say the same thing. Sometimes people tell me that they came to Gloria Dei because they heard it was a place where people really love each other. That means so much to me.

Loving people isn't some kind of weak and mushy thing. It's strong, tenacious, and shows itself most powerfully in the face of rejection. That's how Jesus loves us, and that's his command for us to love each other. In his most famous sermon, he asked, "If you love those who love you, what reward will you get? Are not even the tax collectors doing that? And if you greet only your brothers, what are you doing more than others? Do not even pagans do that?" (Matthew 5:46-47) Instead, he instructs us to love our enemies and pray for those who persecute us. Far too often, I've seen love evaporate in the family of God over a petty misunderstanding. Just imagine what genuine persecution would cause!

> Loving people isn't some kind of weak and mushy thing. It's strong, tenacious, and shows itself most powerfully in the face of rejection.

Jesus outlined the motivation and the measure of our love for each other: "A new command I give you: Love one another. As I have loved you, so you must love one another" (John 13:34). How did Jesus love his disciples? Completely, tenaciously, sacrificially, graciously, and joyfully. They misunderstood him time after time, and they abandoned him in his hour of need. But still, his love never failed them, and it never fails us.

Don't miss the point that our love for others is an overflow of our love for God. The Great Commandment to love God with our hearts, souls, and minds is followed immediately with the second commandment, to love our neighbors as ourselves. The second is the outgrowth of the first. Another perspective on this truth is to note that the *extent* of our love for our neighbor is a demonstration of our *actual* love for God. If we don't love people, then we don't love God, no matter how many praise songs we sing or how much money we give. Paul explained to the Corinthians that love must be real or everything else in our lives is worthless. He wrote, "If I speak with the tongues of men and of angels, but I have not love, I am only a resounding gong or a clanging cymbal. If I have the gift of prophecy and can fathom all mysteries and all knowledge, and if I have a faith that can move mountains, but have not love, I am nothing. If I give all I possess to the poor and surrender my body to the flames, but have not love, I gain nothing" (1 Corinthians 13:1-3). Paul then wrote the most beautiful description of love in the word of God.

What does love look like in real life? It means we move toward people who hurt instead of valuing our own convenience more. It means wrapping our arms around those who struggle instead of rejecting them. It means we ask questions and listen instead of talking too much. Several years ago, I noticed that a lady who had been a part of our church had stopped attending. I saw her one day, and I asked how she and her family were doing. She looked a bit sheepish, like she didn't want to answer my question. I asked, "I was wondering why you stopped attending our church. Did you find one that meets your needs better than ours? If you did, that's wonderful."

She looked even more reluctant now. Then she asked me, "Do you really want to know why we stopped coming?"

"Yes," I assured her. "I sure do."

"I was in a Bible study group," she explained, "and my daughter was having some trouble . . . with boys. She was only 14, but she was sexually active. I mustered up the courage to tell the group about it, and I asked them to pray. But they were aghast. I could feel their condemnation, and I just couldn't stand to be around them. That's why we left, Pastor K."

I expressed my deep sorrow for the way she was treated, and I told her I hoped she would find a place where she felt safe to share her deepest needs. I gave her a hug, and I walked away brokenhearted.

All Christians have feet of clay. We all have sins and situations that bring pain and shame. Because the ground is level at the foot of the cross, there's no excuse for a self-righteous attitude that snarls, "I'm better than you," or "I can't believe you have problems like that! You must be a really bad person." Jesus certainly rebuked religious leaders for unbelief, but he never shamed someone who was hurting. Philip Yancey accurately observed, "Jesus reserved his hardest words for the hidden sins of hypocrisy, pride, greed and legalism." We need to learn that lesson. In Jesus Christ, God has given us—every single one of us—the vast riches of his grace to forgive us and cleanse us. He knows every stinking sin in our lives, but he forgives us. We need to affirm both our desperate need for grace and God's incredible love and forgiveness. We need the reminder, and we need to extend that grace to others.

> We need to affirm both our desperate need for grace and God's incredible love and forgiveness. We need the reminder, and we need to extend that grace to others.

We have a built-in defense mechanism that prevents us from being honest with people about our sins and needs: We simply don't want people to know about the crud in our lives because we're afraid they'd reject us. Recently, I watched a family drive in to our parking lot one Sunday morning. Through the windows, I could see them frowning and barking in anger. They were all furious at each other. They parked a couple of rows over and got out of the car. Now, though, they had on their Sunday smiles! Someone greeted them: "How are you doing this morning?" Both the parents instantly nodded, smiled, and said, "Fine." I hope they weren't fighting again the instant the car doors shut when they left after the service.

Grace operates in an atmosphere of honesty: honest expressions of need and honest displays of love. When that happens, watch out! God will change lives.

TRUST AND RISK

When I was going through a very difficult time in my life and my ministry, I wrote three leaders in our congregation a two-page single-spaced letter telling them, "I'm dying inside, and I need your help." That was a huge risk for me. My father had taught me never to tell anyone about personal problems I might have within the congregation. That information, he insisted, should stay in the family. But God used that letter and those men to help me take steps toward healing and growth.

Today, I meet with five men every Friday morning, and we share our deepest needs and highest hopes with each other. But I'll tell you, even though these guys have proven they are trustworthy, being vulnerable still scares me. Deep in my gut, I'm afraid that if they know who I really am, they'll lose respect for me. That's my risk every Friday morning. To be honest, I don't tell them everything in my heart each week. For one thing, it would take too long, and for another, there are things they simply don't need to know. The principle, though, is that if I need to be held accountable for something, I tell them about it. Each week, we communicate to each other in words, facial expressions, prayers, and consistency that we love each other no matter what. What an ongoing blessing these Friday mornings are to me and my group!

Relationships are based on trust, but trust is often misunderstood and elusive. Some of us trust too much too soon, and we trust even untrustworthy people. Family members of addicts almost always exemplify this problem. The addict lies over and over, but the family member keeps believing, "This time, he'll come through. This time will be different." But it's not. Those who trust too quickly are naïve about people and take unwarranted, foolish risks. They benefit from a hard dose of reality.

On the other end of the continuum are those who are too guarded, too hesitant to trust. Perhaps they've been hurt in the past, and they don't want to risk being hurt again. Some of them isolate themselves from any meaningful interactions with others, and some try to dominate to be sure others can't get the upper hand. These people are unwilling to trust even those who have proven they are trustworthy.

Like Goldilocks and the three bears, some trust too much, some trust too little, but some trust just right. Wise people move toward others with open hearts and open eyes. As I read the Scriptures, I notice that they contain many instructions to "love one another," but there are no commands to "trust one another." Love can be given unconditionally, whether the person deserves

Wise people move toward others with open hearts and open eyes.

it or not, but trust must be earned. Developing trust requires the courage to take small steps of risk and the wisdom to know when to stop. Take steps to be a bit open and vulnerable with an individual or with a small group. If you feel valued and validated, then take another step. When you sense that others feel uncomfortable with your level of vulnerability, stop there and go back a step. You can't insist that people trust each other and go as deep as you'd like. That's their decision, and it's your decision to go as deep as you feel comfortable, too.

The principle of earned trust works in every relationship: at home, at work, in the neighborhood, and at church. For instance, you tell your teenager to be home at 11 o'clock but he comes in at midnight. The next weekend, he expects to be out again, but you say, "Tonight, you have to be in at 10:30 or you'll be grounded next weekend."

Your teenager might react, "What's the matter? Don't you trust me?"

You can respond, "No, I don't. You didn't fulfill your commitment last week, and now you have to earn my trust again."

Any significant betrayal of trust demands that trust be rebuilt. Lying, stealing, adultery, or any other kind of serious relational wound demands time and attention. Restoration can happen, but it's a process of rebuilding trust.

Relationships that grow in the rich soil of trust enrich our lives, but that soil must be tilled, fertilized, and watered. And these relationships aren't static; we have to constantly watch to be sure weeds don't grow and choke out the fruit of love, respect, and trust. All of us are sinful, and all of us wear masks from time to time. Even the strongest relationships have to deal with misunderstandings and hurt feelings. That's normal. Perfection is for another life. A friend of mine talks about "peeling the onion" in relationships. Each layer is another step of the risk of vulnerability and earned trust. Each layer requires courage, and each one promises great rewards.

We don't need a hundred close relationships like this. Just a few enrich our lives beyond measure. Moses had Aaron and Hur to hold up his arms during the battle. David had Jonathan who cared for him in a time of confusion and danger. Jesus chose twelve men, but three, Peter, James, and John, were closer to him than the rest. Paul had Barnabas, then Silas and Titus, to go with him on his mission trips to spread the gospel of grace. All of us need a few trusted friends. Not many, just a few.

> **All of us need a few trusted friends. Not many, just a few.**

We need to recognize our starting point in this journey of trust. Some start by trusting even untrustworthy people, and they need to become much wiser, more reluctant, and selective. Others are too hesitant to trust, and they need to move beyond their fears to reach out to people. All of us, though, are in process. All of us have a lot to learn about loving others the way Jesus loves us. At least I do.

MESSAGES OF GRACE

In his curriculum for men's ministries, *The Quest for Authentic Manhood,* pastor and speaker Robert Lewis defines three messages men need to impart to those in their families.[17] These statements, though, aren't just for men to speak. They are messages of grace for all of us to communicate to those we love in and outside our families. They are:

- "I love you." This message speaks of a person's value or worth. This one seems simple enough, but it is painfully absent from the vocabulary of many believers. Maybe no one said these words regularly when we were growing up. Maybe we're too angry or disappointed in people to utter them. We need to remember, though, that "while we were yet sinners, Christ died for us." God still loved us, so we can love people even if we don't like their behavior.

- "I'm proud of you." This message speaks of a person's character. Notice the positive values in those around you, then name them and nurture them. A friend of mine tells his son in college, "Son, I'm so proud of you for taking a full load of classes, doing well in them, and choosing your friends wisely. That's terrific!" Those words, he told me, are like an elixir to his son's confidence.

- "You're good at_____. I can see you doing_____." The third message is about gifts, abilities, and accomplishments. People need affirmation that we see their existing talents and future potential. These messages help people develop a vision for their lives, and they are essential in instilling courage to take the next step in their lives and careers.

Who should hear these messages? Certainly your family members, but also those where you work or go to school, teachers, friends, and kids in the neighborhood. Be sure to be authentic. People can tell if you mean what you're saying. Some of us need to do a little thinking before we open our mouths to be certain what we say is clear and powerful, especially comments about talents and the future.

> **Be sure to be authentic. People can tell if you mean what you're saying.**

Some of us might want to say, "Well, yeah, I can say these things to others, but what about me? I'd like to hear some of these messages myself." You will. The law of sowing and reaping tells us that we'll reap *what* we sow, *more than* we sow, and *after* we sow. For this reason, you can expect to hear some of these messages with similar or even greater sincerity than you spoke them. (With teenagers, you might hear words of love and affirmation years later. Don't expect a quick return there!)

Many other messages affirm our love for people and confirm the grace and purposes of God in their lives. Sometimes, all we need to tell a hurting person is, "I'll walk with you through this." We can remind people that even when we can't see God's hand at work, he is still fulfilling his purposes. I try to look beneath the surface and imagine what I'd be feeling if I were the person going through celebrations or suffering, and I tailor my words to fit those moments.

On many occasions, those I've tried to comfort encouraged me with their faith in God. When my father found he had lung cancer, the doctors scheduled him for surgery. I remember that day like it was yesterday. My father was on the gurney in the hall waiting to be wheeled into surgery, and I stood next to him. My Dad was a man of few words, but at that critical moment, he looked at me and said, "Son, I'm going to tell you something another father told his son in a similar circumstance: I hope to see you real soon, but if I don't, you know where you can find me." His confidence in his eternal destiny touched me deeply.

Messages of faith, hope, and love aren't optional equipment. All of us need to hear them and speak them—a lot. In my years as a believer, I've come to the conclusion that we simply cannot experience the love of God independently from the love of our brothers and sisters in Christ. How do we know of God's love and strength and kindness? We know these are real when the Spirit of God motivates the people of God to act according to the word of God and touch people's lives with his grace.

People come through the doors of a church because they are looking for something. Some come hoping to belong. Others come with a sense of need. Still others come for unknown reasons, desiring to remain anonymous. Whatever motivates people to come to the church, it's up to us to reach out and understand their needs. Far too often, church leaders put the burden of connecting on the guests. Instead, it's the burden and privilege of church leaders to reach out and embrace people who have already taken the initiative to come to us. Years ago, a couple of people from our church asked me to join a local civic group. I went for about a year, but during that time, nobody else in the club befriended me. Each week, I received a few smiles and handshakes, but no one asked deeper questions or pursued me. I thought I tried to initiate conversation. For some reason, my attempts were not reciprocated. I had some intentions to get involved, and I even volunteered to help on occasion. I would have invested time, energy, and heart into that organization, but after about a year, I gave up. While I accept personal responsibility and possible failure for not connecting better, I believe involvement cuts both ways. I'm afraid many people feel as I did when they come to our churches.

We can't relate meaningfully to 3000 people at a large church, or even to 100 people in a small church. We need a small community so we can really get to know them and they can know us. That's how the church operated in the months and years after Jesus ascended. They celebrated and gathered in the temple and synagogues, but they met deeper needs in their homes (Acts 2:42–47; 20:20). This is why I believe effective small groups are the premiere environments for Christian experience and growth today. Churches have many different formats and curricula for groups. Whatever the system, find one that focuses on Jesus, is rooted in his word, and encourages people to grow in their faith. As people learn to trust each other, these groups can become the most important source of spiritual growth in the church.

Warm, supportive, life-changing groups don't happen overnight. They go through stages of growth, from *exploration* when people are just getting to know each other, to *transition* when each person decides how much they are willing to trust others and be vulnerable, to *effectiveness* when the members celebrate with each other, challenge each other appropriately, and support each other in times of need. At some point, though, the group may *terminate*. It might decide to multiply into more groups so more people can experience the joys and challenges of leadership, or the members may realize that, for whatever reason, their group has run its course.

If you are in a small group, take the initiative to help move the group along to become as effective as possible. If you aren't yet in one, contact your church leaders to find out more about the groups that are available in your area. Don't miss this opportunity to connect with other believers!

THE ART OF LISTENING

Today, our ears are bombarded by more sounds than ever before in history. We seldom escape, and most of us don't want to escape, the sounds of the times. I see people talking on cell phones and listening to iPods when they drive, walk, run, work, play, read, and do practically every other activity. We *hear* a lot, but I wonder if we've lost the art of *listening*.

I know if someone is really listening to me if he asks a second and third question. If he doesn't ask them, I wonder if he heard my answer to the first question! Let me give a few pointers about good listening:

I know if someone is really listening to me if he asks a second and third question. If he doesn't ask them, I wonder if he heard my answer to the first question!

- Pay attention—When people talk, focus completely on them. Do we look at the television or the person walking down the street or anything else when we're in a conversation? Or do we avoid distractions, focus our eyes on the person, nodding when we understand an important point, and looking for hidden clues that might help us understand even better?

- Active listening—Listening requires active participation. Learn to ask good questions, and particularly, invite people to "Tell me more about that." If possible, avoid "why" questions, especially with fragile or angry people because they imply that you demand an explanation. Of course, sometimes you need to ask those "why" questions, but try to ask them later in the conversation after you've listened well for a while and earned their trust.

- Clarifying—Ask a second or third question, and ask people to tell you more about an important point. Mirror the person's feelings, such as, "You felt hurt when he told you that," to give the person permission to be honest.

- Listen with your eyes—Read the person's non-verbal signals to see if the words and actions are consistent. For example, I've talked to couples and heard the husband say, "I love her," but his arms were folded, his brow furrowed, and he leaned away from his wife in his chair. His non-verbals screamed louder than his words! Look for clues in how the person dresses, statements about friends or work, and any other signals that might help you look beneath the surface.

- Don't assume you're clairvoyant!—You may have an intuitive sense that the person is hiding this or that, but be humble and recognize that you could very easily be wrong. I know some gifted counselors who "read" people very well, but even they admit they are wrong from time to time. (By the way, if you are a pastor, keep in mind what a clergy counselor and good friend once told me, "John, never psychoanalyze your wife!")

- Keep confidences—When people trust you enough to confide in you, don't betray that trust by gossiping to others or telling about the person in the guise of a "prayer request." If, though, the person is suicidal or homicidal, tell him you have to tell your pastor or a counselor about it. In talking with teenagers, it's a good idea to tell them that anything they say to you might be reported to their parents. You want to help, but it doesn't help anyone when you get caught in a manipulative triangle.

Listening is an art any of us can acquire. Like any other skill, some of us will be better than others, but all of us need to learn the basic skills that invite people to share their hearts of pain and hope. Love grows when people feel heard.

Love grows when people feel heard.

IN TIMES OF CRISIS

Author and church consultant Lyle Schaller has observed that people grow most dramatically through times of pain. If that's the case, he asks, why do Americans medicate themselves to escape their pain? Certainly, medications can play an important role in helping depressed people think more clearly so they can process their pain, but too often, medications are used to avoid the pain altogether.

Crises are pivot points in the direction of our lives and our relationships. The decisions we make at those crucial times affect us for the rest of our lives. A few years ago, I went to the home of a family that had visited our church. We had a very pleasant conversation, but for some reason, we began talking about death. The mother nodded, "Yes, we know something about death."

"You do?" I asked. "Tell me about it."

She told the story of their four year-old son who had, they thought, a case of the flu. After a few days of care, he didn't improve, so they took him to the hospital. The doctors treated him, and he began to feel better, but suddenly, his condition worsened and he died.

The father told me, "At the time of our son's death, we had to make a decision. We could either allow that tragedy to draw us closer to God or drive us away us from God. We chose to get closer to him, and God brought some wonderful friends along side us to comfort and support us. I don't know what we'd have done without them."

Nobody longs for a crisis. Nobody pursues pain. But for fallen people in a fallen world, stuff happens. Like you, I've seen individuals and families devastated by cancer, accidental deaths, terminal illnesses, Alzheimer's disease, unplanned pregnancies, stillborn children, prodigals, and a host of other problems that devastate people. Those who tried to go through these valleys alone suffered terribly from despair. Those who had the loving support of the

Those who had the loving support of the family of God also suffered, but they experienced comfort, help, hope, and strength so they could cling to God through the most painful periods of their lives.

family of God also suffered, but they experienced comfort, help, hope, and strength so they could cling to God through the most painful periods of their lives.

Rudy Rasmus is the pastor of St. John's United Methodist Church in Houston, a church that has become known for its ministry to the homeless and addicted. Rudy's father once observed, "Church folks only care for you for two weeks." I'm afraid Mr. Rasmus was too often right. In many cases, a small group or a class mobilizes to help people for a couple of weeks. During that time, casserole dishes and pies come by the boatload, but after two weeks, hurting people are often forgotten. Nobody intends to abandon them. We just have other things to do. But long-term problems require long-term strategies for care so that people receive a realistic level of support and don't feel abandoned.

SPEAKING THE TRUTH IN LOVE

Loving people doesn't mean that we affirm every behavior and say nice things when their behaviors are destroying their lives and the lives of others. Sometimes, love must be tough. Even a casual reading of the gospels shows that Jesus was not only the Lamb of God—he was also the Lion of Judah who spoke boldly, sometimes harshly, to those who hurt others. He called the Pharisees a "brood of vipers" and "whitewashed tombs," clean on the outside but full of rottenness and death on the inside.

The Pharisees weren't the only ones Jesus confronted. He didn't ignore Peter's betrayal on the night he was arrested. The risen Jesus confronted the big fisherman and asked three times, the same number of Peter's denials that he knew Jesus, if Peter loved him. In the same way, I know people really love me if they care enough to confront me when I'm headed in the wrong direction.

Speaking the truth in love always is a risk. Several years ago, a good friend asked if he could talk with me after church. As we talked, he quickly got to the point. He told me he had observed some things in my life that concerned him. My anger flared up so much that I couldn't see straight. In fact, the hair on the back of my neck stood up! I thought, "You arrogant so and so!" But in a few minutes, I thought about what he told me, and I realized he was telling me the truth. My initial anger changed to contrition, and God used that conversation to change my life. I am forever grateful my friend loved me enough to speak the truth to me. It took courage (especially when I got so angry), but he weathered the storm, and God used him in a big way in my life. To this day he remains a close friend.

The key to that encounter was the relationship we had developed. In the context of knowing and being known, he saw something in me that needed to change. He had earned my trust, so I was willing to listen. Paul instructed the Galatians, "Brothers, if someone is caught in a sin, you who are spiritual should restore him gently. But watch yourself, or you also may be tempted. Carry each other's burdens, and in this way you will fulfill the law of Christ" (Galatians 6:1-2). My friend fulfilled this command that day. He restored me, and he did it with gentleness. He put the burden of my wrong behavior on his own back, just like Christ did for all of us. The goal of confrontation is not to blast people and vent our own anger at them, and it's not to get more information so we can talk about them behind their backs. The goal, first to last, is restoration and renewal.

He had earned my trust, so I was willing to listen.

SALT AND LIGHT

People are watching. Neighbors, co-workers, and friends are looking at us to see if this Jesus thing is real in our lives. At the end of 19th century, D. L. Moody was one of the leading pastors in the country. He observed, "Out of 100 men, one will read the Bible; the other 99 will read the Christian."

Sometimes, people only get bumper-sticker answers from us like "Jesus is the answer." He is, but religious clichés are not magic potions we dab on gaping wounds. People around us are lost and struggling. They suffer from depression, strained and broken marriages, children who are out of control, mental and emotional disorders, and a host of other disappointments. They are looking for authentic people with an authentic message. They're looking for you and me to represent the love and strength of Jesus Christ to them. That's what it means to be light and salt. Jesus told his men, "By this all men will know that you are my disciples, if you love one another" (John 13:35).

Larry Crabb has said the church should be "the safest place on earth," a place where people trust each other to open their hearts and share their burdens, where God uses the hands, feet, eyes, and mouths of his people to comfort and encourage others. When God's Spirit was unleashed in this way in the first century, the believers "turned the world upside down." The same thing can happen today, but it requires courage to experience and express the love of God in the most joyous as well as the darkest times of our lives.

THINK ABOUT IT

1. Do you agree or disagree with Ney Bailey's statement: "People live for encouragement, but they die without it"? Explain your answer.

2. The foundation of encouraging relationships is our own experience of God's grace.

   — Read 1 John 4:7-12. What are some ways you can love people the way Jesus loves you?

—Read Colossians 3:12-14. How can you forgive others in the same way Christ has forgiven you?

—Read Romans 15:7. Describe some ways you can accept others like Jesus accepts you.

3. Describe a time when you felt most encouraged by other believers. Describe a time when you were hurting, but you didn't feel supported.

4. What are some of the risks in being in a small group? What are some of the rewards?

GOING DEEPER

1. Review the section about "the games we play" in relationships. Do you tend to play any of these games? If so, which ones? What would it take for you to stop playing games and be more authentic?

2. How have you seen God use times of crisis (individual or corporate) to surface needs and build relationships? What was the net result in the lives of those in crisis and of those who cared for them?

3. Read Galatians 6:1-5 and Matthew 18:15-20. Describe the do's and don'ts of confronting someone about a sin.

5. Prayer

THE DOOR OF INTIMACY

"And I will do whatever you ask in my name, so that the Son may bring glory to the Father. You may ask me for anything in my name, and I will do it" (John 14:13-14).

"Oh, if I could only pray the way this dog watches the meat! All his thoughts are concentrated on the piece of meat. Otherwise, he has no thought, wish, or hope." —Martin Luther

God didn't give us prayer to make us feel guilty. He gave it to us so we can connect with him and experience more of his grace and power. For many years, though, pangs of guilt ran through my heart whenever I heard anyone talk about prayer because I was so certain that I was failing God in this aspect of my life. But grace gives us a fresh, new perspective on the discipline of prayer. Grace-filled prayer is the door of intimacy with God.

MYSTERY AND PRIVILEGE

If the White House called me today and asked me to come for a meeting with the President, I'd be really excited. I'd think and plan and dream about the conversation. There are a zillion questions I'd like to ask, but if I'm smart, I'll be a great listener. The President is the one with authority, not I. The President is the one whose position demands the highest respect, not I. But I can go boldly to his office because I am invited. Without that

119

invitation, I have no chance of ever meeting him or developing a relationship with him.

The same is true in my relationship with God, except that God is the creator and ruler of the entire universe, not just a single country on a speck of a planet lost in a vast galaxy in the incomprehensible expanse of all creation. If the President's position demands respect, how much more does the infinite God's? And if meeting with the President is a high privilege, a conversation with God is a thrill beyond measure.

Like other disciplines in our lives, God is the initiator of prayer; we simply respond to him. I wouldn't know to call him "Father" if he hadn't revealed himself to me through his word. And I wouldn't know what was on God's heart if he hadn't shown us his heart in the Scriptures. I have the unspeakable privilege of relating to the divine, but I am painfully human. Too often, I focus on my wants and my needs. Jesus' disciples felt this tension of trying to relate to the divine, and they asked him to teach them to pray. He said, "Pray like this: 'Our Father who art in heaven, hallowed be Thy name. Thy kingdom come, Thy will be done on earth as it is in heaven.' " Jesus' pattern of prayer focuses our attention on God's nature, God's purposes, and God's kingdom. We find our greatest fulfillment when we align our hearts with his, and that's probably the most important role of prayer in our lives. To be fair, Jesus' prayer doesn't only focus on God. It also speaks to our human needs. He says that we must forgive those who have hurt us. We should ask God to provide for our daily needs. Luther observed that this prayer for "daily bread" is answered for every person on earth, not just Christians. We pray that we

> **We find our greatest fulfillment when we align our hearts with his, and that's probably the most important role of prayer in our lives.**

will receive it with thanksgiving. So our part is confession and thanksgiving—a far cry from the self-absorption of many of our prayers—especially mine!

Early in my Christian experience, my concept of God focused far more on his transcendence than his immanence. I had a wonderful relationship with my Dad, but for some reason, that relationship didn't translate easily to my concept of God, who seemed distant and huge. For that reason, I had a difficult time fully understanding God as "Father." I read, though, that Luther encouraged people to think of Jesus as their brother. That really helped me! Now I could go to him as a trusted friend who wanted to know me and be known by me. Of course, God is both transcendent *and* immanent, not one or the other. In our culture, our concept of God has deteriorated into a "good buddy." He isn't that. He is awesome, majestic, and "wholly other," yet still tender and affectionate toward us. We must not lose sight of either his divine or human nature.

The writer to the Hebrews explained that Jesus' humanity gave him complete understanding of our weaknesses, and he encouraged us to respond boldly to God's invitation: "Let us then approach the throne of grace with confidence, so that we may receive mercy and find grace to help us in our time of need" (Hebrews 4:16). But relating to God also involves more than a hint of mystery. In *Reaching for the Invisible God,* Philip Yancey offers an insight about this mystery. He wrote, "In short, God must set the pace of communication, so that we can only know God as he chooses to make himself known. The unequal partnership between the invisible God and material human beings guarantees that much will remain shrouded in mystery. God can know all of us; we can never know all of God. As God himself told Jeremiah, 'Am I only a God nearby and not a God far away?' "[18]

A lady in our church heard me speak on the fact that our faith is rooted in the unseen, the invisible, the intangible. She asked, "Pastor K, what does it mean to trust in a God we can't see?"

121

I remembered a poster that used to hang in our conference room. It read, "Only those who see the invisible can do the impossible." Our task as followers of Christ is to develop spiritual sight so that we believe the invisible world is just as real—maybe more real—than our physical world.

> **Only those who see the invisible can do the impossible.**

When I experienced a very difficult time in my own life, I went to a seminar taught by C. Peter Wagner called "How to Have a Healing Ministry without Making Your Church Sick." I was hoping for God's healing in my own life, and I hoped Wagner could help me. It was a wonderful seminar, but perhaps more helpful was an earlier comment by church growth expert Carl George that prayer is "the atmosphere around us," not an event that punctuates our schedules. In prayer, I breathe in the presence of God and exhale, in confession, the sins and barriers that harm that relationship.

One of the most amazing truths in the Scriptures, and one that I seldom hear anyone speak on, is that our lives are filled, not only with the presence of God, but with the prayers of Jesus and the Holy Spirit. Paul wrote to the Romans, "We do not know what we ought to pray for, but the Spirit himself intercedes for us with groans that words cannot express" (Romans 8:26). And only a few verses later, he tells us, "Who is he that condemns? Christ Jesus, who died—more than that, who was raised to life—is at the right hand of God and is also interceding for us" (Romans 8:34). Can you imagine that? In front of the Father's throne, God the Spirit and God the Son are praying for you and me right now and all the time. You and I may not have a clue what to pray for, but they know fully the will of the Father and pray specifically and constantly about every aspect of our lives. That's mind-boggling.

In 1979, my father had surgery for lung cancer, but soon after the surgery, his health began to decline rapidly. He decided not to have chemotherapy because he wanted to feel as good as possible in his last weeks of life. I asked if we could talk about that decision, and in my father's typical fashion, he looked me in the eye and told me, "No, son. Your mother and I have made that decision." That was the end of the discussion.

As his health deteriorated, I knew God could heal him, and I wanted to pray for that. But my father was 80 years old. How, then, should I pray? If he lived, would he live in pain for a few more years? After wrestling with this issue for a while, I finally prayed, "Holy Spirit, take over. I commend my father and my prayers for him to you. I don't know how to pray, but you know the will of the Father, so I put him in your hands." At that point, I didn't have the burden of figuring out the will of God. This prayer set me free to trust God and love my father in those last days, without the cloud of doubt and guilt.

PERSONALITY AND PRAYER

We've seen in the Scriptures that God created and called each of us, uniquely and specially. He gave each of us a set of talents to honor him, all day, every day, and he shaped our personalities to give us the heart and desire to use those talents. Some of us are bold as lions; some are reflective and intuitive. Some are gifted in gathering people and imparting love to them; some have talents in analysis and systems. We are, indeed, "fearfully and wonderfully made," and quite different from one another. But virtually every time I hear a talk or read a book on prayer, the message seems to come from a reflective, intuitive perspective. I'm a man of action. How in the world do I relate to these messages about prayer and not get frustrated?

I'm a man of action. How in the world do I relate to these messages about prayer and not get frustrated?

In his book, *Invitation to a Journey: A Road Map for Spiritual Formation,* Robert Mulholland explains that God wires each of us differently, and we relate to him the same way we relate to people: actively, reflectively, in community, or in orderly ways. This insight gave me great relief. The same God that created us with differences in our abilities also created us to respond in different ways in prayer. Let me outline some of these differences.

From the time of the ancient Greeks, people have noticed four distinct types of personalities. The Greeks thought these differences came from the dominance of body fluids. In our day, scholars and popular writers identify these four types by using animals, colors, ships, weather, and almost any other rubric you can imagine. One of the most common profiles in existence today is the Perfomax DISC Profiles. Let me briefly describe these and show how each type relates to prayer.

- D's are dominant. They love action and get frustrated with discussions that aren't quick enough and don't result in action. They value relationships that accomplish something together. D's don't like quiet and solitude in prayer. They don't mind praying, but they want to see that it makes a difference. Prayer for prayer's sake frustrates them to death!

- I's love to influence others. They are natural salesmen and coaches who enjoy motivating people. They value lots of relationships, but they don't go as deep in relationships as some others. I's like spontaneity and variety in prayer, and they enjoy praying with others. Like the D's, these people get frustrated when prayer seems too systematic and boring.

- S's are sensitive, reflective people who develop deep, long-lasting relationships. They could sit and talk with a trusted friend for hours, and they are excellent listeners. S's see prayer as a way to connect in rich, meaningful ways with God and to touch the hearts of people they love. Many S's are deeply committed to prayer and devote hours to journaling their thoughts, reflections, and intercession for others.

- C's are consistent people who value systems and organization. They avoid risks as much as possible by ordering their lives in clear, controlled categories. C's focus on God's promises, and they often keep detailed journals of their requests.

I suspect that S's write most books on prayer, and I'm very different from that personality type. For years, I read these books and felt there was something wrong with me, but in recent times, I've realized that I can focus my prayers on seeing God at work in the lives of people around me. My prayers may not be as long or as reflective as someone else's, but they are meaningful to me . . . and I suspect that God delights in my prayers when I reflect who he made me to be.

> **I suspect that God delights in my prayers when I reflect who he made me to be.**

Most people pray best when they are alone and still, but I'm most alert in prayer when I'm active. I like to walk when I pray, or ride in the car, or do something else active. Those things might distract other people, but they are rails for my prayers to run on. Years ago, in his book, *Experiencing God,* Henry Blackaby recommended walking as we pray. When I started doing that, I was amazed. I've never heard the audible voice of God, but when I walk, I often sense the presence and the will of God in a unique way. As I walk, God revs my spiritual engines. He reminds me of things I'd long forgotten and gives me new insights I need for a message or situation.

I used to feel so guilty because my prayer life didn't fit the books I read and the speakers I heard, but then I realized that God wants me—with all the strengths and quirks of my God-given personality—to regularly communicate with him. Today, I have been set free, and I talk and listen to God a lot, and by his grace, I'm often aware of his presence. It's a thrill to delight in God as he delights in me.

HELPFUL PRACTICES

Over the years, I've heard people say thing like, "Journaling (or fasting or solitude or silence or morning devotions or evening devotions or memorizing Scripture or whatever) has revolutionized my prayer life, and you ought to do it, too." I used to feel guilty when I heard those things, then I got angry, but now I am more at ease. Grace really does change things! When we understand that our God-given personalities shape our communication with God, we realize practices in prayer aren't "one size fits all." We can try out a wide range of them and settle on those that fit the way we hear God's voice and relate to him most effectively.

God communicates with us in many different ways: throuh his word, in Baptism and Holy Communion, by the "still, small voice" of his Spirit, through mature believers, circumstances, and the glory of nature. One of the insights that has propelled my own prayer life is the realization that God is constantly attempting to get my attention. It's almost like he's saying, "Pay attention, John. Did you hear what Elaine said?" "Did you see how that situation uncovers a need? I want you to trust me to meet it." "Do you sense the power of the statement Jesus made about what is really valuable in life? John, you need to think about that and make some changes."

Our concept of God filters the messages we hear. In most cases, I hear God encouraging me, directing me, and supporting me as I live for him, but some of us don't sense much encouragement from God. Years ago, I took a group of men on a retreat. During one of our devotional times, we opened the Bible to John 10 and talked about Jesus being the Good Shepherd. I asked them, "How do you see or sense Jesus as the Good Shepherd in your own life?" I thought it was a very easy question that would elicit responses of warmth and affirmation, but almost every man there said that Jesus primarily corrects them. I was astonished. These men, leaders in the church, saw Jesus primarily as an enforcer of rules rather than a caring and loving provider. The picture David painted of God as our shepherd is that he leads us into green pastures and causes our cup to overflow. He anoints our heads with the oil of joy, so that "surely goodness and mercy will follow us all the days of our lives." Does he occasionally correct us? Certainly, but the Good Shepherd delights in his sheep and graciously provides for them. He doesn't delight in catching them doing something wrong so he can blast them! Our concept of God makes all the difference in how we interpret Scripture and how we pray.

The practices of prayer aren't *objects* of worship, they are *means* of worship. They are ways to clear our minds and focus our hearts on God, his purposes, and his direction for us. As we've seen, some of us feel more connected with God

> **The practices of prayer aren't *objects* of worship, they are *means* of worship.**

when we're active, some when we're praying in community, some when we reflect deeply in solitude, and some when we order our prayers. It is vital, though, to find a way to block out the constant noise of life to listen to God. God wanted to speak to his prophet, Elijah. He sent a wind, but God wasn't in the wind. He caused an earthquake, but God wasn't in the earthquake. He sent fire, but God wasn't in the fire. Elijah only heard the voice of God in a whisper. We can't hear God's whisper unless we find a quiet place and a quiet heart. Where is that? For me, walking helps me focus my heart on God. (Unfortunately, I don't walk enough!) Closing my office door and being alone with some of my favorite prayer books also helps. Others benefit from journaling, corporate prayer, and a host of other practices.

I try to read through the Bible on a regular basis, and I try to have consistent daily devotions. I get behind from time to time, and to be honest, I feel guilty about it. (To be Lutheran, I'm convinced, is to feel guilty. Our favorite time of the year is Lent!) I use devotional guides like *By Faith Alone* by Luther and John Baillie's *A Diary of Private Prayers*. These stimulate my thoughts and keep me on track. I set a regular time to think, read, and pray, but I try to stay aware, all day, every day, that I'm in the presence of God.

My parents taught me to pray the Lord's Prayer, Luther's Morning and Evening Prayers, and prayers before and after mealtime. These are powerful patterns of prayer, but these didn't teach me to pray conversationally. For years, I only used only printed prayers, and I was terrified of praying extemporaneously. After I graduated from seminary and entered the ministry, I began to learn to pray spontaneously and conversationally. It has been a wonderful experience, and today, I rarely use printed prayers. The freedom to express my heart to God has become a way of life, and I love it!

The Lord's Prayer teaches us *how* to pray, not *what* to pray. Luther said the Lord's Prayer is "the world's greatest martyr" and "the most crucified" prayer because we often just mouth the words without reflecting on the meaning and letting this prayer become a pattern for our conversations with God. For example, we first reflect on the fact that God is our powerful yet tender Father, and we come to him as beloved children. We then focus our hearts on his purposes and his will, which are effective on earth as well as in heaven. Next we ask God for those things that we need to survive and to serve him, and in that reflection, we are thankful for all he has given us. But we receive those tangible gifts in the same way we receive the spiritual gift of forgiveness, which we extend to those who have hurt us. We ask for wisdom and direction, recognizing that evil is both in the world and in our own hearts. And before we end, we remember again the nature of God, his sovereignty,

> The words of the Lord's Prayer are not the end of our prayers; they are the beginning, the jumping-off point for us to shape our thoughts, praise, and requests as we communicate with God.

power, goodness, and eternity. The words of the Lord's Prayer are not the end of our prayers; they are the beginning, the jumping-off point for us to shape our thoughts, praise, and requests as we communicate with God.

Years ago, I read Lloyd Ogilvie's *Commentary on Acts*. In this book, Ogilvie asked, "Have you ever experienced 'storms in the night'?" Do you ever wake up at night and wonder why you can't go back to sleep? At least some of the times this happens, I believe God wants us to spend some time in prayer." This insight was a revelation to me. Now, when I wake up at night and can't go back to sleep, I don't get angry. I pray, "Lord, I'm awake and you're here. What would you like for me to pray about?" God's Spirit often brings something to mind and burdens my heart to pray for someone or something. For that hour or so, I focus my attention on God's will and ways. I pray for Elaine and my kids, our staff members and people at our church, and usually, I pray for someone who needs God's special touch. When I wake up in the middle of the night, I realize that God is graciously inviting me to talk with him. Those are rich and wonderful times.

My encouragement to you is not to implement a single plan for prayer, but to experiment with a wide range of practices, find some that fit your personality, and use those practices to connect with God in rich, meaningful ways.

OUR "ISAACS"

An evidence of the grace of God in prayer is that sometimes he reveals things that are blocking our relationship with him. That's not surprising. When I've done something that hinders my relationship with Elaine, she tells me about it. When she does, I have a choice to be defensive or to seek forgiveness and restoration. That's God's purpose for showing us blockages in our relationship with him. In my experience, times of prayer are the occasions God often uses to show me those barriers in my relationship with him.

Sometimes, our problems are overt sins of greed, hatred, jealousy, drunkenness, or any other kind of sin that displeases God. For those who genuinely desire to follow God, though, the problem might be very different: holding on too tightly to a possession, a person, or a dream God has given them. They are thankful for God's gift, but sooner or later, the gift nudges God out of the center of the person's heart. Genesis 22 describes this situation. Abraham, the father of our faith, had trusted God (eventually) and God gave him a son, Isaac. The conception was miraculous because both Abraham and his wife Sarah were very old and far past childbearing years. Abraham loved Isaac very much, in fact, he cherished him too much. The boy had taken the place of affection and loyalty in the old man's heart. For everyone's sake, God tested Abraham and forced him to choose between his son and God.

You know the story. God told Abraham to take his son to a mountain and sacrifice him on an altar. I'm sure Abraham was mystified and heart-broken. How could God ask him to do such a thing? Yet the command was unmistakable. Slowly, the old father and young son trudged up the mountain. At the top, Abraham built an altar and gathered firewood. He placed his son on the wood and raised the knife above his head. Suddenly, the angel of the Lord stopped him: "Abraham! Abraham! . . . Do not lay a hand on the boy. Do not do anything to him. Now I know that you fear God, because you have not withheld from me your son, your only son" (Genesis 22:12).

God wants nothing and no one but himself in the center of our lives. He is incredibly patient to nudge us and remind us to choose him above possessions, power, people, and play, but some of us don't get the message. Sooner or later, we may cherish too much the

> **Sooner or later, we may cherish too much the gifts God has given us, and at those moments, he may ask us to sacrifice them.**

gifts God has given us, and at those moments, he may ask us to sacrifice them. He's not being cruel. It's for our own good. If it's children or a spouse, the exercise of moving them from the center of our affections can be excruciating, but they will be the beneficiaries of our refined and refreshed devotion to God. I want to assure you that God will likely never again ask anyone to kill a child, but I also assure you that he will shine his light of conviction on anything that we cherish more than him.

I'm still shocked every time I read the account in Genesis 22 of God telling Abraham to sacrifice his son. Of course, God knew the old man would obey, and God also knew he would stop him. Those of us who walk with God eventually are ordered to take our cherished person or thing to the mountain and remove it from the center of our hearts. These are difficult but cleansing times. Listen to God and respond in obedience and faith. Everyone will be better off for it.

WHEN GOD SAYS "NO"

I've had the pleasure of seeing God perform some incredible miracles, and I thank God for the privilege to witness those events. But sometimes, we desperately want God to show up and work, but he doesn't. Those moments challenge our faith like no other, but even in those times (and especially in those times) we can cling to the inscrutable wisdom and goodness of God. When I pastored the church in Irving years ago, a childhood friend called me with some tragic news. His four year-old son had died. He had taken the boy to the hospital with breathing difficulties, and the doctors performed several procedures that, as it turned out, had contributed to his death. Only hours after the boy died, my friend called me to tell me about the tragedy. He asked, "John, would you come to his funeral?"

Of course, I answered, "Yes, we'll come."

Then he asked, "John, while you're driving, would you pray that God would raise my son from the dead? I believe God can do it."

My heart was stunned. No one had ever asked me to pray for a resurrection before. I stammered, "Yes. I'll ask God to give your son back to you."

On the drive to his house, I prayed as fervently as I possibly could pray, and I knew my friend was praying even more passionately. I thought of instances when Jesus raised Lazarus and the widow's son, and I said, "God, you did it then. Would you do it again now?"

The next day or so, my friend and I kept praying and waiting for God to answer. Then, it was time for the funeral. As we stood next to the casket hovering over the hole in the ground, he told me quietly, "John, you can quit praying for the miracle now. Apparently God doesn't want to raise him from the dead now. However, we both know he'll raise him on the last day."

My friend demonstrated great faith in trusting God to raise his son from the dead, but he exhibited even greater faith in trusting him when God said "No" to his prayers. A man told Jesus, "I believe. Help my unbelief." That's my prayer, too. I believe in God's grace and strength, but I constantly need for God to help me believe him more—especially when he says "No" to me or to someone I love.

HIGHS AND LOWS

I love the psalms because the psalmists were completely honest about their walks with God. Often, they expressed great confidence in God and praise for his glory and grace. But quite often, too, anger and disappointment poured out of their hearts and their quills. They argued with God and accused him of not caring. Many of us feel very uncomfortable saying anything like this to God, but the psalmists didn't seem to have any inhibitions. The point, I think they'd tells us, is that God wants us to come to him and express the deepest feelings in our hearts. He'll sort out the good, the bad, and the ugly. Only in our complete honesty, though, is the opportunity for our genuine connection with him.

An experience of depression taught me more about prayer than anything I've ever encountered. When I was depressed, I no longer had the luxury of self-confidence; I had to cast myself at the foot of the cross, at the place of God's greatest grace. My heart was broken, and I desperately needed God's kindness, healing, and presence. During that time, I experienced "the dark night of the soul," but I also enjoyed an intimacy with God I'd never enjoyed before. In my darkest times, I simply couldn't pray. But as I look back on those times now, I realize that God was, even in the darkness, drawing me into a deeper, more intimate relationship with him.

> **Only in our complete honesty, though, is the opportunity for our genuine connection with him.**

In *The Art of Loving God,* Francis de Sales observed that light is seen most clearly in contrast to darkness. He wrote, "Now the greater our knowledge of our own misery, the more profound will be our confidence in the goodness and mercy of God, for mercy and misery are so closely connected that the one cannot be exercised without the other."[19]

Our society avoids suffering at all costs. That's understandable, but I'm afraid something might be lost in the process. My own grasp of grace was deepened and heightened by my depression, and I'm sure God wants to use struggles in all our lives. Philip Yancey writes eloquently about the presence and purposes of God in suffering. He reflects, "In a culture that glorifies success and grows deaf to suffering, we need a constant reminder that at the center of the Christian faith hangs an unsuccessful, suffering Christ, dying in shame."[20] When we suffer, we can more fully appreciate the sacrifice of Christ, and we grow from the experience.

Some of the doors we face are opportunities, but some are challenges. God gives us—or at least allows us to experience—both, so that we learn to thank him and trust him. James captured the reality of both when he wrote, "Is any one of you in trouble? He should pray. Is anyone happy? Let him sing songs of praise" (James 5:13). Through the ups and downs of my own life, I've learned to look for God's "non-anxious presence." No matter what's going on, no matter how bad things get, God is never rattled. He is in complete control, and he is full of wisdom and strength. As I trust in God and he transforms me more into the likeness of his Son, he offers me his non-anxious presence, and I learn to have confidence in the goodness and greatness of God even in the midst of confusion and pain.

GOD'S PROMISES

I hope these insights about prayer have freed you from any rigid and unfulfilling expectations, so you can respond to God with warmth and joy. Accept your personality and tailor your prayer life to fit who you are. Realize that prayer is a response to God's gracious invitation and his voice. If your prayer life is in the tank, maybe you haven't been listening enough. God has given us precious and magnificent promises to encourage us to trust him. These promises remind us that God may take us through some valleys as well as to mountaintops, but his paths always lead us to a deeper experience of his grace. The best, he assures us again and again, is yet to come.

> **These promises remind us that God may take us through some valleys as well as to mountaintops, but his paths always lead us to a deeper experience of his grace.**

Years ago, I developed a benediction which I often pray to close our worship services. Let me offer this benediction as we close this chapter on prayer:

"May the good Lord go before you to lead you, behind you to encourage you, beside you to befriend you, beneath you to uphold you, above you to protect you, and within you to inspire you. Go in the peace and power of Almighty God."

THINK ABOUT IT

1. What are some reasons it's important to remember that God is the initiator in prayer? What might happen if we think we have to carry the conversation all the time?

2. Can you identify and describe your personality type? What are some ways an understanding of personality and prayer frees you to pursue God more?

3. Which practices of prayer are most meaningful to you? Explain your answer.

4. Read the Lord's Prayer in Matthew 6:9-13. Take some time to paraphrase it and pray your version to God. Which aspects of this pattern of prayer are most meaningful to you? Explain your answer.

GOING DEEPER

1. Has God ever shown you an "Issac" in your life that he wanted to deal with? If so, how did you respond, and how did that experience free your heart to focus more on Christ? If not, identify possible "Isaacs" that can take the place of Christ in our hearts.

2. What have been some highs and lows in your walk with God? How has God used both to encourage you to praise him and depend on him more?

3. What are some "precious and magnificent promises" in the Scriptures that encourage your faith and prayers?

6 · Bible Study

THE DOOR OF INSIGHT

"When your words came, I ate them;
they were my joy and my heart's delight,
for I bear your name" (Jeremiah 15:16).

"It's not what I don't understand about the Bible that bothers me;
it's what I do understand!" —Mark Twain

*A*s you can tell from reading this book so far, we talk a lot about grace at our church. One Sunday morning after the service, a young man came up to me and asked, "Pastor K, I like what you say about grace, but I've been wondering. If God forgives us and accepts us no matter what we do—that's grace, isn't it?—then why can't I just go out and do whatever I want to do? You know, live it up!"

That's a great question, and it's one people have been asking since Jesus' day. Chuck Swindoll has said that grace is "dangerous" because of the stunning freedom it gives. It is so dangerous that it can be misused and abused, but God would have it no other way. God is unwilling to limit his grace just because we might misuse it. That's the depth of his love and the depth of our freedom to respond to him. The Bible tells us all we need to know about God's marvelous grace and his purposes for us. The Bible is the door of insight for any of us who are willing to turn the handle and walk in. We begin to mine the riches of God's word by understanding law and grace.

BOTH SIDES NOW

When I was in high school and college, people told me I needed to go to seminary and become a pastor, but I wanted to be a teacher like my Dad. I graduated from Concordia Teacher's College in River Forest, Illinois, seven years after one brother, fourteen years after another brother, and forty-four years after my father graduated from that school. In one of my courses on the teaching of religion, the professor assigned us to read an article on the distinction and correlation of the biblical teaching of law and grace (gospel). The founder of the Lutheran Church-Missouri Synod wrote the article many years ago. Studying that article changed my life.

Law, the article told me, always commands, prohibits, requires, and renders judgment. When we read passages of law, God uncovers and identifies sin in our hearts and deficiencies in our character and actions. Grace, on the other hand, always promises, forgives, and reassures. The ultimate purpose of the law is not to leave us beaten and bloody, full of guilt and shame. The purpose of the law is to expose our desperate need for grace. Exposure of our sinfulness forces us to be honest about the darkness in our hearts. Proper, biblical guilt is the knowledge that we need forgiveness, and we turn to Christ for his cleansing. Conviction hurts, but shame destroys. Shame is the result of denying our sins and trying to overcome them with rituals and good deeds. Those efforts, the Bible assures us, don't work. The only solution for sin is God's grace, not our penance. Paul explained the difference between conviction and shame: "Godly sorrow [conviction] brings repentance that leads to salvation and leaves no regret, but worldly sorrow [shame] brings death" (2 Corinthians 7:10).

When the law says, "You shall not covet," and the Holy Spirit convicts me of envy, I have to respond, "Lord, you're right. I am greedy and envious. I want things I can't have, and that's sin. I need your forgiveness."

I may want to water down the law of God, but I can't. It stands tall and strong as a tower of truth. I don't like what it says about me or to me, but I sure like where it leads me—to the cross of Jesus Christ where I find love, forgiveness, and freedom from my guilt.

Before someone trusts Christ as Savior, he may look at the law and conclude that it is harsh, demanding, and even cruel, and, at that point, it is. But looking back at law from the position of grace, we see law as a necessary guide to lead us to grace. As believers, we now know that the law continues to protect us from ruining our lives and tarnishing our witness to those who need to know Jesus. The law doesn't cease to exist when we become Christians. Instead, it takes on an important role of guiding us as we strive to do God's will.

> I don't like what it says about me or to me, but I sure like where it leads me—to the cross of Jesus Christ where I find love, forgiveness, and freedom from my guilt.

The young man's question was, "Why don't we misuse grace and sin all we want?" The answer is that grace is more than freedom. It is a relationship with someone who loves us more than we can possibly imagine. If we grasp even the smallest aspect of that immense love, we will want to please him in every possible way. We don't *have* to do the right thing, but we *want* to do it because we love the one who set us free.

STANDARDS, BENCHMARKS, AND GUIDELINES

Our conscience is one of the marks of "the image of God" in us. Except for psychopaths, every person has a God-given instrument in our hearts that signals right from wrong. Certainly, that instrument is tarnished, but it still operates. Both nature and nurture play a role in shaping our sense of values and the sensitivity of our consciences. People develop many of their values, though, from their environments. I believe that the model of our parents is perhaps the strongest force in shaping our lives. God created the family as a gift to teach, model, correct, and challenge children to follow him. But as we all know, parenting isn't an exact science. Some of the best and godliest parents I know have a prodigal child, and some children of abusive or neglectful parents turned out to be wonderful young adults. But the principle of "not falling far from the tree" rings true in most of our lives. Historian David McCullough noted that as President of the United States, Theodore Roosevelt often found himself in difficult situations. On those occasions, he habitually asked himself what his beloved and wise father would do.

Our culture tries to shape us into its mold. The preponderance of messages about the value of possessions, pleasure, and pleasing people threatens to drown out the whisper of God's Spirit in our lives. In America, we value "rugged individualism." Our standard for what is right is what makes us feel good. The benchmark for our decisions is simply, "Do I want to do it?" And the covers of magazines, the ads on television, and the mannequins in store windows shape our standards.

But there's another standard for us to measure life: God's word. The Bible is criticized for being an ancient book, written by a score of farmers, shepherds, and kings, to a culture that hasn't existed for a long time. Yes, it's an old book, but I'm amazed that the insights in the Bible are as fresh and clear today as they were when they were written, thousands of years ago. How can that be? Because the character of God and human nature haven't changed one bit.

For generations, people scoffed at the Bible because they couldn't fit the history in the Scriptures with the writings of ancient historians. In the last few decades, though, archeologists have found thousands of artifacts, tablets, and ruins that confirm the history depicted in the Bible. Luke's gospel and his account of the early church in Acts were especially suspect, but recent findings have proven, over and over again, in minute detail, that

Luke's history of governors, rulers, cities, and cultures is incredibly accurate. We can trust the Bible for two reasons: internal evidence and external evidence. It speaks clearly and powerfully to man's condition with a consistent message. It has been validated by scholars and archeologists, many of whom initially set out to disprove the Bible, but became believers when they came face to face with the overwhelming evidence of its validity.

Paul tells us, "All Scripture is God-breathed" (2 Timothy 3:16). The Greek word Paul used is *theopneustos,* which reminds us of God breathing life into Adam's nostrils when he created him in the Garden. When Paul wrote these words, the entire Old Testament, but only part of the New Testament, had been penned. But Paul is affirming that God himself breathed life into the Scriptures. He guided those who wrote the words, so that we might understand God's divine nature and God's gracious message to us. Because it is from the mouth of God, the words are authoritative for faith and life. To the Romans, Paul wrote, "Faith comes from hearing the message, and the message is heard through the word of Christ" (Romans 10:17).

Centuries ago, Puritan pastor Stephen Charnock observed that many believers were "practical atheists," who attended church, but whose lives had not been transformed by God. I wonder what Charnock would say about our culture today. As the culture has drifted more toward worldliness and selfishness, we desperately need a fresh respect for God's word.

I have high regard for God's word, and the biblical authors wrote passionately about the value of Scripture. The Lord spoke

> **It has been validated by scholars and archeologists, many of whom initially set out to disprove the Bible, but became believers when they came face to face with the overwhelming evidence of its validity.**

to Joshua after the death of Moses and told him, "Do not let this Book of the Law depart from our mouth; meditate on it day and night so that you may be careful to do everything that is written in it. Then you will be prosperous and successful" (Joshua 1:8). David trusted God's word to guide and direct him. He wrote, "Your word is a lamp to my feet and a light to my path" (Psalm 119:105). To the prophet Isaiah, the Lord said,

"As the heavens are higher than the earth,
> so are my ways higher than your ways
> and my thoughts than your thoughts.
As the rain and the snow
> come down from heaven,
and do not return to it
> without watering the earth
and making it bud and flourish,
> so that it yields seed for the sower and bread for the eater,
so is my word that goes out from my mouth:
> It will not return to me empty,
but will accomplish what I desire
> and achieve the purpose for which I sent it"
> (Isaiah 55:9-11).

In the New Testament, Jesus himself affirmed the authority of Scripture over and over again. He said, "Heaven and earth will pass away, but my words will never pass away" (Matthew 24:35). God wants us to grow in spiritual maturity, and we can't grow apart from the truth and grace we find in his word. Paul scolded the believers in Corinth who hadn't grown as much as they should have: "Brothers, I could not address you as spiritual but as worldly—mere infants in Christ. I gave you milk, not solid food, for you were not yet ready for it. Indeed, you are still not ready. You are still worldly. For since there is jealousy and quarreling among you, are you not worldly? Are you not acting like mere men?" (1 Corinthians 3:1-3) Paul expected more from those who had listened to the word of God for a long period of time, and I suspect he would expect more from most of us, too.

ALL OF GRACE

Seen properly, the Scriptures are all about grace from beginning to end. We often think of the Ten Commandments as rigid, condemning rules, but as we've seen, God uses them to expose our need for our Savior's grace. God spoke the first commandment: "I am the LORD your God, who brought you out of Egypt, out of the land of slavery. You shall have no other gods before me" (Exodus 20:2-3). No other gods? In the Garden, Eve was deceived by Satan, but Adam sinned willfully. They both chose to turn their backs on God because they wanted "to be like God" instead of loving and serving him. I'm the same way. The selfishness and evil in my heart focus my desires on me. No one else, just me. Left to myself and apart from God's redemption, I am the most selfish person in the world. That hard reality drives me again and again back to the heart of God for forgiveness and refreshment. I have nothing to offer God. I come empty handed. John wrote, "This is love: not that we loved God, but that he loved us and sent his Son as an atoning sacrifice for our sins" (1 John 4:10). How wonderful! His grace frees me and encourages me to love him more than ever.

Martin Luther saw grace in these commandments. His commentary on the first commandment reads: "What does this mean? We should fear, love, and trust God above all things." In fact, all of Luther's explanations of the Ten Commandments begin with the phrase, "We should fear and love God so that . . ."[21] All of these commandments, and, indeed, all the commands of the law throughout the Scriptures, point us back to the awesome nature of God that should inspire us to fear, love, and trust in him. The Ten Commandments offer us ten wonderful gifts. They

> **The Ten Commandments offer us ten wonderful gifts. They guard us, direct us, and warn us to cling to the God of forgiveness, love, and wisdom.**

guard us, direct us, and warn us to cling to the God of forgiveness, love, and wisdom. What better gift could we ever receive?

Some people think that the two parts of the Bible are contradictory, but that's simply not true. The New Testament is hidden in the Old, and the Old Testament is revealed in the New. The same God of law and grace reveals himself in both. We just need eyes to see him.

I've heard people describe characters in the Old Testament as "perfect" and models for us. Well, when I read about Abraham, I see his faith, but I also see years of doubt and his difficulty handling conflict in his family. Jacob's band of twelve sons included Joseph, a model of strength and wisdom, but the rest of them were liars, cowards, and attempted murderers. And King David? He was a great leader and "a man after God's own heart," but he was also an adulterer and murderer, a man who wasn't a good father for his children. Eventually, he paid the price for his parenting mistakes. The characters in the Old Testament were sinners in need of a Savior, just like us. They trusted God's promise to send one. We look back in history at that Savior, but we're all on level ground at the foot of the cross.

THE POWER OF THE WORD

After Paul told Timothy that the Scriptures are "God-breathed," he describes the way God uses the Bible to change our lives. He wrote that the Scripture "is useful for teaching, rebuking, correcting, and training in righteousness, so that the man [and woman] of God may be thoroughly equipped for every good work" (2 Timothy 3:16-17).

This passage tells us that understanding and applying God's truth includes four elements, which we can articulate in four questions:

Teaching: What does this passage teach me?

When we look at a passage of Scripture, we want to know what it tells us about God, about people, about relationships, about money, or about whatever topic it addresses. Read verses in context to see where the author was coming from and where he was going. For example, the most abused text in the Bible is Philippians 4:13: "I can do everything through him who gives me strength." I've heard athletes use this to say God will help them win a game, and I've heard people in the business world claim it as a promise of success in a business deal. The context is Paul explaining that he can find contentment whether he has a lot of food or very little! The verse has nothing to do with winning games or making deals.

Read the context and ask simple questions—who, what, when, where, why, and how? If it's a difficult passage (or even if it's not) ask, "What was the author trying to say to his original audience? How would they have understood this passage?"

We need to be careful that we don't read our own values and ideas into the Bible. I love the cartoon I saw years ago of a little girl peeking into a room where her brother was reading the Bible. The boy told her, "Don't bug me, sis. I'm trying to find some verses to support my preconceived ideas!"

Rebuke: How do I fall short of this truth?

This question opens the door for God's law to do its work. For example, when I read that God wants me to be kind, the Holy Spirit often reminds me of conversations when I was abrupt or too busy to care for a person in need. The Scriptures have incredible power to see deep into our hearts and reveal hidden selfishness. The writer to the Hebrews wrote, "For the word of God is living and active. Sharper than any double-edged sword, it penetrates even to dividing soul and spirit, joints and marrow; it judges the thoughts and attitudes of the heart. Nothing in all creation is hidden from God's sight. Everything is uncovered and laid bare before the eyes of him to whom we must give account" (Hebrews 4:12-13).

When I recognize sin and shortcomings in my life, I don't have to wallow in shame and self-pity for hours or days to "feel bad enough long enough" to pay for the sin. That's completely unnecessary, and it's impossible. Furthermore, it's an affront to the grace of God that forgives freely and completely. As we become more confident of God's grace, we'll become more open to his rebuke as he shows us sins that displease him. We are wise to be honest and say, "Yes, Lord, you're right. That's sin." That's confession which frees us to receive absolution and empowers us to make amendments or changes in our lives.

Correction: What am I going to do about it?

Paul told the Ephesians, "If you're lying, stop it. If you're stealing, quit doing it." In most cases, the correction we need to make is crystal clear. But sometimes, the sin is of the heart, not the hands, so the correction has to be made in our attitudes. In these cases, my correction is to reflect more on the goodness and purposes of God, so my heart can be transformed.

Our identity as children of God is the springboard for right thinking, good attitudes, and godly behavior. Paul wrote to the Colossians, "Therefore, as God's chosen people, holy and dearly loved, clothe yourselves with compassion, kindness, humility, gentleness and patience. Bear with each other and forgive whatever grievances you may have against one another. Forgive as the Lord forgave you. And over all these virtues put on love, which binds them all together in perfect unity" (3:12-14). Paul focused their attention on their identity as "chosen, holy, and dearly beloved" as the motivation to live in a way that reflects that identity.

> **Our identity as children of God is the springboard for right thinking, good attitudes, and godly behavior.**

Training in righteousness: How can I make this a discipline in my life?

A deed done once does not make a discipline. People *fall into* bad habits; Christians *cultivate* disciplines. For good choices to sink deep into the fabric of our lives, we have more work to do. If we're watching too much television, we need to avoid the room where it's on and buy a good book to read, find a hobby that interests us, exercise, or find friends to spend time with. And we need to put these things into our schedules, so we don't drift back into old habits. Instead, we work on our disciplines.

I believe every Christian needs an accountability partner. This person may be in a small group with you, have breakfast or lunch with you once a week, or talk with you on the phone. This person can ask searching and fearless questions to keep us on track with our commitments. I meet with a group like this every Friday morning, and I treasure our time together. These men keep me on track when all kinds of stresses and temptations try to move me in the wrong direction. They help train me in righteousness.

SOME HELP

Let's be honest: The Bible is a daunting book. When new believers pick it up, many of them give up before they even begin because the task of understanding it seems hopeless. Let me offer some practical suggestions to help you wade into it, soak up the truth and grace you'll find, and allow God to use it to change your life.

- Find a version that's easy to read. Don't just dust off the 20-pound Bible that's been in the closet since Woodrow Wilson was President. Bookstores have lots of translations that are easy to read. In this book, I've used the New International Version. Many people enjoy *The Message,* a paraphrase of the Bible by Eugene Peterson. You can look up various translations and paraphrases online to see how they read, but don't stop looking until you find one that you enjoy reading. I believe that modern translations make good study Bibles, while those that paraphrase God's word help our devotional lives.

- Luther said that reading the Bible is like picking apples. We should pick the low hanging fruit first and struggle to get the rest later. Many people pick up the Bible and start (like they'd start any book) with Genesis, chapter 1, with the intention of reading straight through. Most of them make it through Genesis without much trouble (lots of great stories there!), but they get bogged down a few chapters into Exodus. And let me assure you, if Exodus doesn't get them, Leviticus surely will!

I encourage you to begin with one of the gospels, the life stories of Jesus. I believe a good one to start with is the gospel of John, the fourth book in the New Testament. Then read Romans. Next read several of Paul's letters to churches: Galatians, Ephesians, Philippians, and Colossians. If you are new to the faith, or have limited experience in reading the Bible, don't spend much time on complex or confusing books like Leviticus, Daniel, or Revelation. You'll find plenty of transforming truth in the gospels, the letters of Paul, and a few other books, like Psalms and Proverbs.

- This should go without saying, but I'll say it anyway: Go to a church where God's word is valued and taught. Be wary of churches which only give lip service to the Scriptures. They don't treasure the truth, so they don't mine it for hidden gold. Look for a pastor who loves to study God's word and who explains it in a way that is both encouraging and challenging.

- Attend a Bible study group. Participate in a church which has small groups, Sunday school, or other classes which teach the word of God. Make time to go so you can soak up the truth. Ask questions, and study the assignments. It's not just homework—it's life-changing communication from the Savior!

- Pray for an open heart. Before you open God's word, ask the Holy Spirit to give you insight and the courage to apply what you learn. Our study of the Scriptures should refresh our hearts with God's great grace, but God wants "all of me, all the time." And his purposes are far bigger than anything

I can imagine. I'm constantly challenged by the awesome nature of God and his desire for me to participate in his work on earth.

- Blend prayer with your Bible study. As God shows his truth to you, take that truth to his throne and talk to him about it. Quite often, as I study, people and situations come to mind, and I stop and pray for them. That's not wasted time! It's time well used! It makes my study of Scripture rich and real.

- Find a time that works for you. I'm not talking about rigid legalism; I'm suggesting that the things we value most find a way into our calendars and schedules. If you learn to treasure God's word, you'll carve time out of your busy schedule and invite him to speak to you through your study. Some people find mornings are best; some like to read and study just before they go to sleep at night. I know some people who like to study the Bible at work—during breaks, that is! It doesn't matter. God is available and waiting for you, all day, every day. Find a time that works for you and regularly feast on his word.

- Look for answers to your heart's needs. I've heard that "worry is concern that hasn't said its prayers," but worry also is concern that hasn't found encouragement from God's truth. Paul told the Philippians, "Do not be anxious about anything, but in everything, by prayer and petition, with thanksgiving, present your requests to God. And the peace of God, which transcends all understanding, will guard your hearts and your minds in Christ Jesus" (Philippians 4:6-7). In my experience, my prayers are shaped and sharpened by the truth of God's word. This is why I often "pray scripture," because there I find hope, comfort, peace, and courage to face the situations and people in my life.

- Let your heart and mind steep in God's truth. Paul wrote the believers in Colossae, "Let the word of Christ dwell in you

> **Then the Holy Spirit can bring that passage to mind anytime, anywhere to encourage and guide you.**

richly as you teach and admonish one another with all wisdom" (Colossians 3:16). As you read a passage several times, you might just find that you are, believe it or not, memorizing it! Then the Holy Spirit can bring that passage to mind anytime, anywhere to encourage and guide you. Many people have affirmed the value of memorizing Bible verses, telling me that they have spoken God's word to themselves as they approached surgery. I'm not the greatest at memorizing Scripture, but I can tell you that my efforts have been well worth it.

- Respond with courage. Whatever the passage tells you to do, do it. If the Scriptures talk about reconciliation and you're at odds with someone, take steps to restore the relationship. If it says to be self-controlled, stop with one serving of dinner and go for a walk. If it says to be humble, be honest about your sense of pride and your defensiveness when someone disagrees with you.

  Let me give you a warning: If you develop a habit of *not* responding to the word, Bible study will become dry and boring. Read the psalms to see the passion of people who were honest with God and responsive to his Spirit. Then, go and do the same thing. Develop the discipline! Ask God to give you direction as you read his word, and then make a commitment to act on what you read. I often pray, "Lord, make your desire for my life my desire."

- Expect God to speak to you. In the pages of the Bible, we find all kinds of people, in all types of situations. Many of them cried out to God, and God made himself known to them. In John's opening paragraphs, he calls Jesus "the Word," because it is God's very nature to communicate with us. As you read God's book, expect him to open your heart to reveal himself and his will to you.

BURNING HEARTS

After the resurrection, Jesus appeared to many different people on several occasions. On the evening of his resurrection, he appeared to two men as they walked along the road from Jerusalem to the village of Emmaus, but they didn't recognize him. The two men were confused. They had thought Jesus was going to become a great leader, but instead, he'd been killed. They had heard that he had been raised from the dead, but, understandably, they had a hard time believing that report. Now, as they walked along the road, the unknown traveler listened to them as they poured out their shattered hopes. Then he spoke to them, "'How foolish you are, and how slow of heart to believe all that the prophets have spoken! Did not the Christ have to suffer these things and then enter his glory?' And beginning with Moses and all the Prophets, he explained to them what was said in all the Scriptures concerning himself" (Luke 24:25-27).

The three men arrived in Emmaus and had dinner together. As Jesus took bread, gave thanks, and broke it, the men recognized him! Then he disappeared. "They asked each other, 'Were not our hearts burning within us while he talked with us on the road and opened the Scriptures to us?'" (verse 32)

Burning hearts. That's the power of God's word when the Holy Spirit uses it to speak to our deepest needs and highest hopes. When we grasp the truth of grace so deeply that it overwhelms our sense of shame, our hearts burn with thankfulness. When we realize that God's purpose for us is to partner with him in the greatest enterprise the world has ever known, our hearts burn with passion to honor him. Bible study need not be dull—it can still produce burning hearts.

I love the Scriptures because they reveal the heart of God to me. Again and again, the Bible reminds me that, in spite of my sins, God loves and forgives me for Christ's sake. No matter how many times I've messed up, God isn't finished with me, and no matter how long I've walked with him, the best is yet to come.

THINK ABOUT IT

1. Explain why we should fear God's perfect law and why we should treasure it.

2. How do you think your parents have shaped your concept of God and your view of truth? How do you think our culture has shaped them?

3. Read one of these passages, Colossians 3:12-17, Romans 12:9-21, or Matthew 16:24-27, and answer these questions:
   — Teaching: What does this passage teach me?

   — Rebuking: How do I fall short?

   — Correcting: What am I going to do about it?

— Training in righteousness: How do I get this into my daily schedule?

(If you have time, do the same exercise with other passages.)

4. Review the "helps" at the end of the chapter. Which of these suggestions would help you most? What do you need to do to make this happen?

GOING DEEPER

1. Which passages of Scripture has God used most powerfully at pivotal times in your life? How did he use them either to convict you of your sin or convince you of his forgiveness?

2. Read Hebrews 4:12-13. Describe a time when God pierced deep into your heart to convict and transform you.

3. Have you ever experienced a burning heart as you've studied God's word? If so, describe that time.

7·Service

THE DOOR OF FULFILLMENT

"However, I consider my life worth nothing to me, if only I may finish the race and complete the task the Lord Jesus has given me—the task of testifying to the gospel of God's grace" (Acts 20:24).

"There is always the danger that we may just do the work for the sake of the work. This is where the respect and the love and the devotion come in—that we do it to God, to Christ, and that's why we try to do it as beautifully as possible."
—Mother Teresa

*B*ob Buford owned a cable television company, and God richly blessed his business. Wealth and power, however, didn't fill the hole in Bob's life. He had a nagging sense of emptiness, so he went to a psychiatrist. Bob shared his dilemma, and the psychiatrist told him, "Bob, I want you to go home and take out a piece of paper and a pen. Draw a box, and in that box write the words that describe the most important thing in your life. Then come back and let's talk about it." Bob went home, prayed about it, and finally decided to write two words in that box. The two words? *Jesus Christ.* Bob has shared this story countless times, and on each occasion, he relates that this simple exercise transformed his life. Why? Because every person longs to live for a great cause, and the greatest cause in the world is Jesus Christ.

We say we want to "be more like Jesus," but what does that mean? Certainly, one of the main characteristics of Jesus was his servant's heart. In Matthew's gospel, Jesus explained the upside down nature of authority and service in God's kingdom: "Jesus called them together and said, 'You know that the rulers of the Gentiles lord it over them, and their high officials exercise authority over them. Not so with you. Instead, whoever wants to become great among you must be your servant, and whoever wants to be first must be your slave—just as the Son of Man did not come to be served, but to serve, and to give his life as a ransom for many' " (Matthew 20:25-28).

Jesus is the ultimate servant. If we want to be like him, we'll learn to serve with a dynamic blend of gladness and passion, and we'll find the role where we can be most effective in building his kingdom. When our hearts are full of God's grace and we see him using us to change lives, we experience genuine delight.

PASSION AND FIT

As people come to visit Gloria Dei, they often remark that they've never seen so many people serving—and serving with so much joy! That thrills my heart. Many churches are like football games, with a large number of people sitting and watching, and a very few exhausted people doing all the work! That's not the way it's supposed to be. Two things are essential for people to serve joyfully: passion and fit.

Paul wrote often about his passion for serving Christ, and he made it crystal clear that the source of his motivation was the incredible grace of God. In his second letter to the believers in Corinth, he explained, "For Christ's love compels us, because we are convinced that one died for all, and therefore all died. And he died for all, that those who live should no longer live for themselves but for him who died for them and was raised again" (2 Corinthians 5:14-15). He made choices every day to live wholeheartedly for Jesus Christ for the single, compelling reason that he was overwhelmed by Christ's sacrifice for him. Nothing else came close. Throughout his letters, we find Paul referring to the awe-inspiring grace of God as his foundation and source of joy and strength.

Paul's identity was completely defined by his relationship with Jesus. Before Jesus confronted him on the road to Damascus, Paul was a religious zealot, but he spent his zeal against Jesus. After that life-changing encounter, Paul channeled his passion to live for the one who had died to set him free. And Paul saw every moment, every encounter with people, and every situation as possibilities to advance the cause of Christ. That's what he lived for.

The same grace that motivated Paul to love and serve Jesus Christ is the grace that motivates you and me—it's no different. As you and I are overwhelmed with God's love, forgiveness, and purpose for our lives, we'll do everything to please him and expand his kingdom. We won't need to be prodded or cajoled. Nothing can hold us back! When we see needs, we'll dive in to meet those needs. Sooner or later, we'll realize that God seems to use us more powerfully in one role or another, so we'll settle into that role so we can be as effective as possible. Fit, though, follows passion. We can serve even if we don't fit that well, but without passion, we won't want to serve at all . . . or not for very long, anyway.

> The same grace that motivated Paul to love and serve Jesus Christ is the grace that motivates you and me—it's no different.

LIVING FOR THE CAUSE

We've all heard that we need to live "a balanced life." In most cases, that's completely true. In eating, sleeping, working, and every other part of our lives, we need to maintain a sense of balance. But the Scriptures never say our love for Jesus should be "balanced." No, it should be extreme, passionate, and overwhelming. The flame of our love for him should be so hot that every other relationship—and certainly, our love of every possession—is cool in comparison. And our love for people should be pretty warm! But we can't manufacture this kind of love. It comes from a rich, strong, authentic experience of God's love and grace in Jesus. This kind of passion can't be tacked on the outside; it has to overflow from our "innermost beings."

Confidence in our role, however, may not come until we've served for a while. A few years ago, a lady came to me with a suggestion that the church should start a ministry to moms. We met and talked about the idea, and it sounded like a ministry that would really help a lot of women. I told her, "This sounds great! Who's going to lead it?"

She shook her head and said, "Pastor K, I don't know. I thought you'd find somebody."

I smiled, "Well, maybe I did. How about you?"

She shook her head and frowned this time. "Noooooo, I don't think so! I just can't be a leader."

I asked, "Would you be willing to give it a try?"

She thought for minute and then nodded, "Yes, I guess I can do that, but I'm not guaranteeing anything."

That dear lady had the courage to do something she'd never done before, and God used her to develop a wonderful ministry. She recruited women to help, equipped them, encouraged them, and together, they have touched a lot of lives. She hadn't seen herself as a leader, but she became a fantastic one. Confidence followed courage.

Confidence followed courage.

In his letter to the Philippians, Paul stated simply, "For me, to live is Christ" (1:21). What does it mean for us to live for the greatest cause in the world, Jesus Christ, and his redeeming purpose? It means several very important things:

We learn what real life is about.

People live for all kinds of things today, but almost all of them boil down to a common denominator: self. Human nature screams to us that we simply have to have success, pleasure, prestige, and approval to be happy. Virtually every advertisement in every form of media plays on this deception. Toothpaste ads tell us that the product will not only make our teeth white, it will win us the approval—and even the affection—of those we want to impress. Credit card companies promise to make our lives far happier because we can get whatever we want whenever we want it. How self-absorbed can we get? And beer ads . . . let's not even go there. But all of those promises are lies. The product or service may do what they say it will do, but the implication is far beyond white teeth, oiled engines, and clean toilet bowls. The underlying promise is that these things will fill the hole in our hearts and give us what only God can provide. And we've believed them.

One of the most important—and most elusive—lessons we'll ever learn is that our attempts to grab as much pleasure, prestige, people, and possessions as possible ultimately leave us shattered. Only one can fill the hole in our hearts. Only one can illuminate our minds. Only one can make our lives ultimately meaningful: Jesus Christ. He is the source and the secret of life. Do we want treasure? Paul told the Colossians that his purpose was to help people have "the full riches of complete understanding in order that they may know the mystery of God, namely, Christ, in whom are hidden all the treasures of wisdom and knowledge" (2:2-3).

We live fearlessly.

When Paul wrote, "For me, to live is Christ," he continued, "to die is gain." He had no fear of death. In fact, he looked forward to it because it meant he would meet Jesus face to face and spend eternity with him! The conflict in his heart wasn't the fear of death. Instead, his tension was that, though he longed to be with Christ, staying alive meant that he could share the gospel with more people. He concluded, "Convinced of this [the value of spreading the gospel], I know that I will remain, and I will continue with all of you for your progress and joy in the faith, so that through my being with you again your joy in Christ Jesus will overflow on account of me" (Philippians 1:25-26). Do you see both sides? Dying meant he would be with Jesus, free from sin and enjoying perfect delight in Christ's presence. But living provided him the opportunity to serve Jesus a little longer and share his grace with more people. Either way works. Either way is fearless.

Many of us are afraid of death, and some of us are genuinely terrified of it. To be sure, those who don't know Christ have good reason to fear, and I pray their fear will prod them to consider the grace of God. But those of us who know Jesus personally as our Savior and Lord need to examine the magnificent promises throughout the Bible that our eternity is secure. It will be a place that is more wonderful than anything we can possibly imagine. In his book, *Heaven*, popular author and speaker Randy Alcorn wrote, "I imagine our first glimpse of Heaven will cause us to [sic] gasp in amazement and delight. That first gasp will likely be followed by many more as we continually encounter new sights in that endlessly wonderful place. And that will be just the beginning. . . ."[22]

> **But those of us who know Jesus personally as our Savior and Lord need to examine the magnificent promises throughout the Bible that our eternity is secure.**

Jesus promised to "prepare a place" for his followers, and he promised they would be with him for all eternity. There, all tears will be wiped away, and his people will experience more joy, love, challenge, and fulfillment than they ever dreamed possible. Will we trust Jesus' word about heaven and about what has value during our time on earth? If we trust him, we'll live fearlessly.

We believe every problem is a possibility in disguise.

When Paul wrote to the Philippians, "To live is Christ and to die is gain," he wasn't sitting at the beach with a glass of lemonade in one hand and his pen in the other. He was in jail, and he wasn't sure if the next time that door opened it would signal the end for him. But uncertainty, false accusations, and even the ridicule of fellow believers didn't blind Paul to the reality that God was still at work. He wrote, "Now I want you to know, brothers, that what has happened to me has really served to advance the gospel. As a result, it has become clear throughout the whole palace guard and to everyone else that I am in chains for Christ."

First, Paul was thrilled because the guards chained to him were a "captive audience" who had to listen to him tell them about Christ. Then, he states, "Because of my chains, most of the brothers in the Lord have been encouraged to speak the word of God more courageously and fearlessly." His example was a model for a lot of other believers, and they began to share the gospel with passion. I'm sure they thought, "Hey, if Paul can do it in prison, we can do it while we're free!"

But a few misguided believers used Paul's predicament to try to gain prestige in the church. He observed, "It is true that some preach Christ out of envy and rivalry, but others out of goodwill. The latter do so in love, knowing that I am put here for the defense of the gospel. The former preach Christ out of selfish ambition, not sincerely, supposing that they can stir up trouble for me while I am in chains. But what does it matter? The important thing is that in every way, whether from false motives or true, Christ is preached. And because of this I rejoice" (Philippians 1:12-18).

How's that for a good attitude? How's that for seeing God's possibilities when others saw only problems? We don't wait to serve God until we have everything in place and our lives are all together and going smoothly. No, we love him and serve him, all day, every day, through the joys and

How's that for a good attitude? How's that for seeing God's possibilities when others saw only problems?

disappointments, when people understand and when they don't. Ultimately, we serve because we want to please the one who rescued us and showered his affection on us. His grace motivates us—and that's enough.

We major on the majors.

We live in the age of possibilities. A couple of generations ago, women got married and kept house, cooking, cleaning, and ironing each and every day because it took that long to get their work done. Men worked from sun up to sun down six days a week, and still had to milk the cows on Sunday. From the time they were old enough to walk, children pitched in wherever they could help. All of life was consumed with survival.

Today, though, life is different. We can't even keep up with all the new conveniences that come out every year. Technology promises to make our lives easier and more fulfilling. It has accomplished the first, but it has failed in the second. We have far more time and money than our grandparents, but our time and energies have been absorbed by a myriad of non-essential things: shopping, video games, movies, sports, television, etc. In our wealthy, fast-paced, consumer-oriented culture, we have to focus our energies even more on the things that are really important. If we don't, our time will be consumed on second-rate things, and we'll waste the opportunities God has given us to make an impact for him.

Priorities—that's what I'm talking about. We—I certainly include myself in this admonition—need to step back. We need to take a good, hard look at what's important in life, and reconstruct our lives with a refreshed passion to please God. We need to take our schedules and checkbooks to the throne of grace and ask, "Is this or that use of time and money fulfilling my purpose to honor God?" "Is this pursuit getting me where God wants me to go?" "Is the time I'm putting into this organization providing a place to win people to Christ, or am I here just for selfish reasons?"

We are naïve to think that we can simply add Jesus to our existing set of desires and pursuits. He doesn't want to be an addition to our lives. He wants to be in the absolute center, where his interests become our interests, where what breaks his heart breaks our hearts, and where what thrills him thrills us. That's majoring on the majors.

FIND A GOOD FIT

Sometimes when I talk with volunteers who serve God at Gloria Dei, their eyes light up when they tell me how God is using them. They describe the thrill of seeing children grasp a principle from the Bible, helping an elderly person get to church, serving someone in need, welcoming someone who is looking for a church home and has come for the first time, or a thousand other roles people play. With obvious excitement, a man told me about the way God was working through him. I observed, "You love it, don't you?"

He replied, "Pastor K, I was made for this!"

If we have a passion to serve God, we need to find a role where we can channel our efforts. We don't need a *perfect* fit, just a *good enough* fit. As we serve, God will enable us to sharpen our skills or move us to a role we fit even better. Finding the right role takes some time and attention, and it requires that we become good students of our resources. Many church leaders have written

> **"Pastor K, I was made for this!"**

excellent books on serving God. Rick Warren has made a great contribution with his writings on "SHAPE," and we have adopted many of his insights here at Gloria Dei. However, I want to use the word "SERVE" as an acronym for the elements of a good fit.

Spiritual gifts

God has given all believers talents and abilities to be used to honor him. The Scriptures contain four passages that list and describe these "spiritual gifts": Romans 12, 1 Corinthians 12, Ephesians 4, and 1 Peter 4. These lists, though, aren't consistent and are not meant to be exhaustive. For that reason, I believe we can have a broad view of our God-given abilities, and virtually any talent can be used in God's kingdom. In the letter to the Corinthians, Paul clarifies the source and the purpose of the gifts: "There are different kinds of gifts, but the same Spirit. There are different kinds of service, but the same Lord. There are different kinds of working, but the same God works all of them in all men. Now to each one the manifestation of the Spirit is given for the common good" (1 Corinthians 12:4-7).

A friend of mine is skilled at woodworking. Years ago, he was fascinated by carpenters and cabinetmakers, and he wanted to try his hand at it. He bought some inexpensive tools and some wood, and he found some plans and began the project. Through trial and error, he learned a lot in that first venture. His mistakes only made him more committed to learn as much as possible so he could do a better job the next time. Over the years, his skills have developed, and today, he is known as a master craftsman.

My friend's experience is similar to any of us who serve God. We don't become effective instantly by magic. Three things are required: an initial interest, the initiative to give it a try, and honing the skills God has given us. Then, when we find what we do really well, we'll look for the best opportunities to serve.

Some church leaders distinguish between "spiritual gifts" that function in the church and "other talents" that are used outside the church. I don't find this dichotomy helpful because it can too easily extend the sacred/secular distinction. I believe God wants to use the abilities he's given us 24/7, on Sunday morning at church and on Tuesday afternoon at work or at home, all day, every day. Some churches suggest that someone is "serving" only if they are active in a church's ministry. In my opinion, whatever God has led you to do, both inside and outside of the church, if you do it for his honor and in his name, it's serving him. That's good enough for me. It's not one or the other—it's both/and.

I believe if enough people have that attitude, we won't have to worry about finding enough ushers on Sunday mornings.

Experiences

Our desires and talents have been shaped by all the experiences of our lives. Our family background shaped our values, and even if we experienced abuse or abandonment, the hard lessons we learned through those times are invaluable. Education, work, relationships, health, and all the other aspects of life built us into the people we are today.

Most of us have used different types of personality profiles to help us find the best fit for our personalities, talents, and experiences. One type of instrument, however, focuses on past successes as predictors of future effectiveness. One, called a MAP®, for Motivated Abilities Pattern[23], asks people to reflect on experiences, from their childhood to the present, and identify times when they felt fulfilled and successful. The pattern of these experiences usually includes many different types of events and relationships from each period of life, but when they are compiled, they reveal a fairly consistent picture of the activities that brought fulfillment and success.

My life has been shaped very positively by my relationships with my parents and siblings. Their love gave me a solid foundation and the confidence to step out and take risks for God's kingdom. As I look back at the experiences that have given me joy, they have come in every stage of my life, but they all center on leading people, communicating, and building organizations. That's what revs my engines, and that's how God has used me. A pretty good fit, don't you think?

That's what revs my engines, and that's how God has used me. A pretty good fit, don't you think?

Relationships

One of the main reasons so many people enjoy serving God in our church and our community is that serving is infectious. As I look at the Scriptures, I see Jesus inviting people to join him, Paul asking Barnabas to come along, and the first set of deacons banding together to serve God. In the body of Christ, we need to follow their example and invite people, "Hey, come with me!" I believe most people will be thrilled to join us. As people see us enjoying serving with so much enthusiasm, lots of people will want to come along.

Even in the most functional roles, like setting up chairs or doing other manual labor, it's a lot more fun to do it together with a team spirit. Ministry leaders need to capitalize on our God-given desire to be in community. Even if a task involves a lot of individual work, like folding and stuffing a mailing, they can create a warm, encouraging team environment so that people feel they are part of a family. That kind of leadership makes a difference—a big difference—in people's attitudes and joy in serving.

We become like those we hang around. In some cases, that's pretty scary, but if we find a role with people who are walking with God, it's a beautiful thing. Solomon wrote, "He who walks with the wise grows wise, but a companion of fools suffers harm" (Proverb 13:20). Serving God can be one of the most positive, dynamic, life-changing experiences of our lives if we partner with men and women who are sold out to Jesus Christ. And maybe people will benefit from hanging out with us, too.

Vitality

As we've seen, a passion for Jesus Christ is the first and foremost criteria for service, which produces a sense of vitality and the joy of life. What do you see when you look at volunteers (or church staff) in the church? Do they have a look that says, "I can't believe they'd let me be a part of this! I love it!" or do their expressions communicate boredom, guilt, or fatigue?

Vitality comes from the powerful combination of genuine passion, God's calling, and a "good enough" fit. We don't have to have perfect roles, but we need to serve in roles that match our desires, abilities, and opportunities. Ralph and Jean Barkin came to me with a desire to start a ministry to senior adults in our community. They said, "Pastor K, we believe God is calling us to start this ministry. We don't know where to begin, but we want to get going."

I told them, "Great! Go for it! Let me know what you need, and I'll get it for you. And check with me from time to time to let me know how things are going."

Ralph and Jean sensed God's compelling call, and they began that ministry. Today, several hundred people are involved, receiving care and encouragement, and having a lot of fun, too!

Transformation comes when people sense God's call to serve. Some of them realize they've been gifted for a particular role, and some simply realize a need must be met and they can meet it. Sometimes, like when Hurricanes Katrina and Rita ripped through the Gulf Coast and people flocked to our city for shelter, the need is so massive that people want to do anything they can to help. That's

Transformation comes when people sense God's call to serve.

what happened here at Gloria Dei. Those weeks after the hurricanes were some of the most hectic in our church's history, but God brought us together in wonderful ways to serve shoulder to shoulder to meet the needs of strangers. And many of those strangers have become friends.

If you are a church leader, be careful not to over-challenge or under-challenge someone. For some, ushering is a perfect fit, but for others, meeting 50 new people—and being nice to them—is a big stretch. Don't assume you know what's best for someone. Take time to ask questions and listen to discern the person's passions, experiences, and desires.

From time to time, people need a break. A man served faithfully and gladly for many years, but when his father developed Alzheimer's disease, he needed to spend more time with his dad. For a few months, he tried to do everything he had been doing at work, at home, and in the church, plus his additional responsibilities with his father. As we talked, I assured him that he wasn't disappointing God by spending time taking care of his father, and in fact, this was the service God wanted him to perform at this stage of his life. The tension in his heart dissolved, and he took a break from his church service to focus his time and attention on his father.

Many different stresses—some unexpected, some predictable—interrupt our lives and cause us to step back to reassess our commitments. We are complex creatures with many needs, varying capacities, and different abilities as we walk through the stages of our lives. God's first priority is that we love him with all our hearts and love others as ourselves. Sometimes, we have to *step out* for a while before we can *step up* again.

Excellence

Serving God isn't a "throw in." We don't decide to serve him only if we can't think of something else to do. When we are gripped by the grace of God, we'll want to use every fiber of our being to honor him, and that zeal will show up in a commitment to excellence. I'm not talking about perfection. That comes in the next life. All Christians are in process; we're both fallen and redeemed, so nothing we do on this side of eternity will be perfect. A commitment to excellence isn't a guilt trip. Not at all. It's a desire to have all our efforts reflect the goodness and greatness of God.

Strangely, most of us pursue excellence at work or in hobbies without any hesitation, but when it comes to God, we get weird and imagine that we have to be perfect to be acceptable. Others, though, see serving God as optional and unimportant. God wants our best efforts, not our afterthoughts. He doesn't want us to use a few scraps of time between "really important" things. He wants us to use some of our best time to think about, pray about, and plan our service so we can be as effective as possible When we pray, we pray fervently; when we sing, we sing with gusto; when we serve, we want it to touch people and change lives. We've looked at Paul's directives to slaves in his letter to the Colossians. Remember what he said? He wrote, "Whatever you do, work at it with all your heart, as working for the Lord, not for men, since you know that you will receive an inheritance from the Lord as a reward. It is the Lord Christ you are serving" (Colossians 3:23-24).

Paul is reminding us that our service isn't for a church, it isn't for a pastor, and it isn't even ultimately for the people who benefit from it. It's for Jesus Christ. His grace sets us free from guilt and perfectionism, but his grace also compels us to serve him with all our experience, all our talents, and every ounce of desire in our hearts. That's a commitment to excellence.

> His grace sets us free from guilt and perfectionism, but his grace also compels us to serve him with all our experience, all our talents, and every ounce of desire in our hearts. That's a commitment to excellence.

A FEW SUGGESTIONS

I'm well aware that people reading this book fall across the entire spectrum of experience in serving God. Some have recently tasted the grace of God, and they are so thrilled that they are willing to sign up to do anything for him! Some have been sitting in the stands watching a few tired players in the game, and it's time for these people to come down and join them. Some are serving in roles that aren't quite right, and they need to find a better fit. And some wake up each day with a deep sense of gratitude that

God allows them to partner with him in the greatest adventure the world has ever known! Wherever you are at this point in your experience, let me offer a few suggestions for you.

Affirm that God has a terrific plan for your life.

He created you and shaped you with good experiences and bad. All of those experiences give you either confidence or compassion, and you'll need both to be effective in serving him. You are "his workmanship, created in Christ Jesus for good works." The question isn't *if* God has a place for you to serve. The question is *where.*

Reflect on your SERVE to see where you can serve most effectively and gladly.

Look up the passages of Scripture, talk to a mature Christian friend, and ask God to guide you in the next (or first) step in finding a role that fits you. Ask God for clear direction and a sense of his calling to a particular role, where your passion to serve and opportunity meet.

Some have asked, "Should I wait until I have a real desire to serve, or should I just jump in and see what happens?" That's a good question. Psychologists have debated for the past few decades about the connection between feelings and action. Do we feel our way into actions, or do we act our way into feelings? I don't think it's either/or, but both/and. Paul told us, "Your attitude should be the same as that of Christ Jesus" (Philippians 2:5), and then he paints a vivid portrait of Christ humbling himself to serve us. A few verses later, he tells us bluntly, "Work out your salvation with fear and trembling" (2:12). Start where you are. Consider the example of Christ, and ask God to give you a taste of his attitude of humility and servanthood, and then look for a place to dive in and serve. Realize that your first attempt is not likely to be where you end up in a few months or a year, but get up, get going, and watch God use you in others' lives.

If you've tried to serve before, but it didn't work out, don't give up.

Talk to your pastor or another leader in the church. Explore roles that excite you, and see if one of them is available. There's nothing magical in finding a good fit, and God hasn't promised it will happen instantly. Like any skill, yours will need to be developed, and all organizations (even the church) require time and attention to recruit, select, place, train, and shepherd people in their roles.

From 1964 to 1966, I taught the 3rd, 4th, and 5th graders at our church school. I did a good job—which means I didn't kill any of them! The tension I felt each week (to say nothing of the nervousness of a few of the parents) soon let me know that I needed to do something else to serve God. I soon discovered that God created me with abilities to lead and teach adults. I'm thrilled that God has called some wonderful people to teach and lead little kids, but I'm also thrilled that I'm not one of them! I don't feel guilty about that fact. That's just the way God wired me. I have found great fulfillment in pastoring a church.

> There's nothing magical in finding a good fit, and God hasn't promised it will happen instantly.

If you're burned out, take a break.

There's nothing evil or wrong with being tired, and there's nothing wrong with needing to make an adjustment for a while. You might just need a week or two to get your mind right again, or you may need extended time away to focus on other priorities. Talk to your ministry leader, explain the situation, and find a competent replacement. God will provide.

Expect God to work.

God is in the business of changing lives, and he's given us the unspeakable privilege of being his partners in this venture.

As you jump in and serve in some role, expect God to use you to touch people's lives. As you pass the offering plate, realize that God is using you in a sacred contract between himself and each person who puts a check or cash in the plate. As you care for children, take meals to someone who is sick, move chairs, teach a class, comfort a grieving person, put up posters, and do a hundred other jobs in the church or the community, open your eyes to see God at work through you.

Before long, you'll see God work in your own life. You may have begun with some fear, but now you experience great joy. As you serve, passages of Scripture that used to sit on the page now leap into your heart. Your times of prayer become richer and more meaningful because you are aware of specific needs and you trust God to meet them. And your relationships with others will grow and develop as you serve together.

If you are a ministry leader, recruit, select, and train wisely.

Many factors shape people's direction for service. They may start out in one role but soon realize they fit better somewhere else. Give grace, be flexible, and encourage people a lot! Churches are to be communities where God's grace abounds. Businesses can be rigid and demanding, but even there, the culture seems to be changing. Peter Drucker once commented that the function of the church is not to become more business-like. Instead, the function of the church is to help businesses become more church-like. So, let's be church-like, remembering that people thrive on encouragement, but they die without it.

A friend of mine told me that his father joined a Methodist church in Georgia when my friend was about eight years old. His father had been in the Navy in World War II, and he was a stereotypical sailor. He drank and cussed; in fact, almost everybody in the town was surprised when he joined the church. One leader in the church, though, didn't get the whole story. The next Sunday, he asked the new member to be a greeter. That next Sunday, my friend's dad stood faithfully on the front steps of the church welcoming everybody with friendly greetings, "Damn, it's good to see you!" "Hell of a nice day, isn't it?" Recruit, select, and train wisely. Enough said!

Reflect often and always on the grace of God.

Guilt and obligation motivate people, but not for long. I've seen far too many people grind out their service in churches where leaders pressure them to serve. I hope that's never the case here at Gloria Dei, although I'm afraid it has occurred even here.

Grace is the fuel for our zeal, comfort in times we mess up, and the joy of our hearts, all day, every day. A friend once told me, "No matter how long I've been a Christian, I've always been amazed by the cross." That's the way it ought to be.

> Grace is the fuel for our zeal, comfort in times we mess up, and the joy of our hearts, all day, every day.

The church is an organization of sinful people, trying to cling to God and serve him the best they can. If we don't keep the cross of Christ central in our minds, we can drift away into lethargy and quit, or we can try to build a monument to ourselves. Neither of those touches people with the grace of God.

I thoroughly enjoy leading men and women, boys and girls, to know and follow Jesus Christ, but our church isn't about me, and it isn't about anybody else in the church. It's about Jesus. He's the one who thrills us, comforts us, and directs us. We live to serve him.

Years ago, I carried more of the burden of ministry than God intended. I guess I wanted people to look up to me as much or more than they looked up to Jesus. I put in long hours—from six in the morning until midnight, seven days a week. I was consumed by all the needs in the church, and I sweated all the small stuff. During that time, I generally drove my staff and myself nuts. (It was a wonderful time!) I told my brother Melvin about all my troubles, hoping he'd feel sorry for me. Instead, he looked at me and said, "John, you've forgotten who is the real Messiah. You can't save the world. Only Jesus can."

His insight cut me to the heart. Today, I tell people if I have an "S" on my chest, it doesn't stand for "Superman." It stands for "Stupid."

No one is disqualified.

Many people who are new to the church (and a few who have been around a while) think that they can't participate in serving because they, well, aren't perfect like they should be. As I look in the Scriptures, I'm encouraged that God used, and continues to use, flawed people. Abraham and Sarah were old and doubted God's promise. Isaac's son, Jacob, was deceitful. Moses was reluctant to obey God, even though God appeared to him in a burning bush. Gideon was timid; Samson was impetuous and foolish, and David committed adultery and murder. Jesus' followers didn't fare any better. Peter denied him, and Thomas doubted. Paul captured and killed Christians before he met Christ. All of these people and many others in the Bible were deeply flawed, but God still used them to carry his message and build his kingdom.

All of us are flawed, and all of us need the grace of God. Our experience of his grace is what sets us apart, energizes us, and gives us courage. Paul wrote to Titus: "For the grace of God that brings salvation has appeared to all men. It teaches us to say 'No' to ungodliness and worldly passions, and to live self-controlled, upright and godly lives in this present age, while we wait for the blessed hope—the glorious appearing of our great God and Savior, Jesus Christ, who gave himself for us to redeem us from all wickedness and to purify for himself a people that are his very own, eager to do what is good" (Titus 2:11-14).

That's the heart of a grace-filled servant. That's the person I want to be, and I'm sure that's the person you want to be, too.

THINK ABOUT IT

1. Read Philippians 2:1-11. What are some of the motivations Paul gives for us to serve Christ humbly and gladly?

2. What are some causes your friends live for? How do those causes affect them? What are some ways that making Christ our compelling cause helps us live fearlessly?

3. Examine the elements of SERVE. Which of these do you have the best handle on? Explain your answer. Which one do you need to work on? What are some steps you need to take?

4. Evaluate your current role in serving God. What do you enjoy most? What frustrates you? What do you need to communicate to your ministry leader so you can serve more effectively and passionately? What is one thing you can do to be more effective?

GOING DEEPER

1. If someone were interviewing you, how would they evaluate your level and quality of passion and fit in your current role in service?

2. Does the encouragement to pursue excellence inspire you or scare you? Explain your answer.

3. How do your church leaders respond to people who:
   —aren't serving at all?

   —aren't fulfilled in their role?

   —feel burned out?

   —are serving gladly and faithfully?

8· Giving

THE DOOR OF AUTHENTIC FAITH

"But just as you excel in everything—in faith, in speech, in knowledge, in complete earnestness and in your love for us—see that you also excel in this grace of giving" (2 Corinthians 8:7).

"We make a living by what we get, but we make a life by what we give." —Winston Churchill

Years ago, when I began a series on stewardship at Gloria Dei, I entertained the thought of starting by asking everybody who doesn't tithe to stand up. Since I'm alive and writing this book, you know I didn't ask it!

People act strangely when pastors talk about giving. If we preach on the cross, the glory of God, or almost any other topic, Baptists say, "Amen, brother!" Charismatics stand up, raise their hands, and shout, "Hallelujah!" And Lutherans exhibit their usual emotional outburst of a faint smile and a slight nod. When we talk about giving, though, many people take personal offense and treat us like we're pushy used car salesmen.

To be fair, some people have listened to a few preachers who give used car salesmen a bad name! They use guilt and manipulation to pressure people to give. Maybe the budget was short that month, or maybe they just never connected grace and giving in their own lives. Whatever the problem, they missed giving their people a tremendous source of joy. Joy? Yes, joy. A life of generosity brings joy to our hearts as we see God use our resources to change lives. What a privilege!

The habit of giving generously and cheerfully is both a response to the grace of God and a reminder of God's gracious provision in our lives. People who give have an authentic faith, and those who are learning to give are growing in their authenticity. In the last chapter, I wanted to honor the people of Gloria Dei for their hearts of service. In this chapter, I want to honor the people of our church for their incredible generosity. As I write these words, faces flash in my mind, men and women, young and old, whose love for God is genuine and pours out from their hearts and their checkbooks. Many of them give so much so often that it humbles and inspires me. I am deeply grateful for these wonderful people.

ALL ABOUT GRACE

In this book, we've seen that we pray in response to God speaking to us, we study the Scriptures in response to God's initiative to communicate with us, we build relationships with others because God has adopted us into his family, we share the life and message of Christ because he has given us a new identity, and every other discipline is a response to God's initiative of grace in our lives. Giving is no different. We give out of hearts that overflow with gratitude for God's great grace. If we've experienced even a taste of his love, forgiveness, and strength, we won't grouse about giving. Instead, we'll be thrilled to participate with God in his great work!

Many passages of Scripture give us encouragement to give, and in fact, Paul devotes two chapters in his second letter to the Corinthians to this important subject. We'll spend a lot of time there in this chapter. Let me share a few insights that keep us on a strong foundation of grace.

God owes us nothing, but he gives us everything.

Paul described the heart of grace in giving when he wrote, "For you know the grace of our Lord Jesus Christ, that though he was rich, yet for your sakes he became poor, so that you through his poverty might become rich" (2 Corinthians 8:9). We can't twist God's arm, and we have nothing in our hands to use as bargaining chips. We can't show him how good we are because he knows far better than we do that our hearts are wicked, sinful, and self-righteous. That's why we needed grace in the beginning, and why we still need it, all day, every day, for the rest of our lives. Before God, we were like Untouchables with leprosy in India, nothing to offer, with no hope at all, desperately poor and needy.

But Jesus stepped out of the fabulous glory of heaven into time and space, emptied himself, and became poor so he could shower his riches in grace on you and me.

You and I are stinkin' rich! And we did nothing to earn it.

You and I are stinkin' rich! And we did nothing to earn it.

God owns it all.

This principle strikes at the heart of our selfish nature and our consumer culture. The most popular and descriptive word in our language is "my." We love to possess things, and the more we possess, the more we can play the one-up game with our friends. We can't be happy until we have a bigger house, a nicer car, a faster boat, and fancier clothes than the next person, so competition and comparison consume our thoughts.

God spoke to the people of Israel through the psalmist:
"Hear, O my people, and I will speak,
O Israel, and I will testify against you:
I am God, your God.
. . . for every animal of the forest is mine,
and the cattle on a thousand hills.
I know every bird in the mountains,
and the creatures of the field are mine.
If I were hungry I would not tell you,
for the world is mine, and all that is in it"
(Psalm 50:7, 9-12).

> **The concept that everything in the universe was created by God and is owned by him shatters our self-absorption.**

The concept that everything in the universe was created by God and is owned by him shatters our self-absorption. Those things we treasure so much aren't ours at all. They are God's, and he's just loaned them to us for a while. We are stewards of the riches, resources, and possessions he has entrusted to us, and like any steward or manager, someday we'll give an account.

Grasping the fact that God owns it all helps me open my hand and present to him all that he has given me. I tell him, "Here, Lord. All this is yours. What do you want me to do with it?" That prayer is a far cry from daydreaming all day about getting more and bigger stuff! And knowing that God owns it all helps me when I'm shopping because I realize that many of the things I buy, I just don't need at all. That money could be used much more powerfully in other ways. Don't get me wrong. I'm not advocating asceticism, and I'm not suggesting that we become monks and nuns and give away all our possessions. God wants us to enjoy his great gifts, but he also wants us to use them with an eye on him and his kingdom.

God wants us to partner with him in the greatest enterprise in history.

When Paul wrote to the believers in Corinth, he expressed his joy for their generosity in contributing to his ministry. Through their giving, they became partners with God and with Paul. They were so eager to be partners that they "urgently pleaded" with Paul to let them join in. Paul relates, "For I testify that they gave as much as they were able, and even beyond their ability. Entirely on their own, they urgently pleaded with us for the privilege of sharing in this service to the saints" (8:3-4).

The principle is simple, but church leaders need to ask: Do people sense that it is a great privilege to partner with us as well as with the Lord? The Corinthians felt that way about Paul, so they gave for two reasons: to honor God and to help Paul in his ministry. Their joyous generosity overwhelmed and surprised Paul. He commented, "And they did not do as we expected, but they gave themselves first to the Lord and then to us in keeping with God's will" (8:5).

Have you ever seen pictures of starving people in a Third World country and thought, "How sad. Too bad we can't do much of anything about it"? But is it true that we're helpless to meet that need? A fascinating article about John and Sylvia Ronsvalle, the founders of *Empty Tomb, Inc.*, in Champaign, Illinois, tracked consumption and giving patterns of Americans and American Christians in light of desperate needs around the world. In "The State of Church Giving Through 2003," the Ronsvalles assert, "If members of historically Christian congregations in the U.S. had given at the 10% level in 2003, there would have been an additional $156 billion available. The potential impact of this money is seen in need statistics that could be addressed in Jesus' name: $5 billion could help stop the majority of 29,000 deaths a day around the globe among children under five, most of whom are dying from preventable poverty conditions; $7 billion could provide basic education for the world's children; $124 million could launch a massive word evangelism effort in the '10-40 Window' (area of global need)."[24] I find these statistics to be staggering, don't you? And especially so in light of Jesus' comments that "inasmuch as you have done it for the least of these my brothers, you have done it for me."

Too often, we excuse our selfishness and blind our eyes from the needs of others. We think, "Hey, I deserve everything I've got, and I want a whole lot more!" Or "I can't give anything. I don't have what I want yet." Or "I worked hard for my money. I'm sure not going to give it away!" Or "Hey, their problem is not my problem. Let them work for what they need. I've got enough to worry about."

For many of us, money and possessions are the measuring stick of our identity. The more we have, the more we can wield power and win approval. But as we've seen, Christians have a very different measuring stick: an identity rooted in Christ's grace, and an open hand holding the things in our lives. As Christians, we are either good ambassadors or bad ones, strong partners or weak ones. We have a choice each day to say "Yes" to God and work with him in every way to reach people with the gospel, or to say "No" to him and live self-centered lives.

God wants to show us that he will provide for us in tangible ways.

The Christian life isn't just a philosophy. It's a relationship with a living God, who makes spiritual truth a reality in our physical world. Our use of money is at the heart of our lives, and God wants to use money to show us that he, indeed, is Lord of all. Some of us have a very difficult time believing that we can give to God with the confidence that he'll provide for our needs. But that's his promise.

> **Our use of money is at the heart of our lives, and God wants to use money to show us that he, indeed, is Lord of all.**

I could tell story after story of people who chose to give because they realized they are stewards of all God had given them, and God richly blessed them for giving. In a few cases, people gave sacrificially, like the widow that Jesus pointed out to his disciples who gave all she had to live on, and God miraculously provided for these people. When we write the check, we are saying, "God, thank you for making me a steward of some of your riches. I trust you to provide for me and my family, and I delight in being your partner in reaching the lost, building the church, and sending people around the world to tell others about you." We trust him to provide, and he delights in our faith.

God wants us to experience greater joy.

Throughout these two chapters in Paul's letter to the Corinthians, he expresses joy and thankfulness, and he calls his readers to join him in outbursts of joy. Giving, he assures us, is "an act of grace" in response to God's generosity to us. We delight in the opportunity to give because "God is able to make all grace abound" to us. And seeing lives changed through our gifts causes our hearts to "overflow in many expressions of thanks to God."

Generous people are joyful people. Stingy people are self-absorbed, angry, and resentful people. Which kind of person do you want to be?

Jesus said more about money than any other topic. He talked about people and their relationship with their possessions more than heaven, more than hell, more than the Second Coming, more than family relationships, more than humility, and more than faith. Money, he knew, is central to our perspective on every other aspect of life. If the grace of God penetrates our view of money and possessions, it will permeate every relationship, every desire, and every decision. Our use of money reveals our hearts more clearly than any other aspect of life. The German pastor, Helmut Thielecke warned, "Our pocketbooks can have more to do with heaven, and also with hell, than our hymnbooks. He who has ears to hear, let him hear!"

A man in our church was a very successful businessman. He built a large company and made a ton of money. Though he came to church regularly, he didn't seem to connect with the message of grace. One year, we participated in a nation-wide outreach. Our church conducted some Bible studies in conjunction with this effort, and I preached weekly messages. Week after week, he came and listened very intently. At the end, he announced at a banquet where we celebrated our successful effort, "Now I know what Jesus meant when he said, 'It is easier for a camel to go through the eye of a needle than for a rich man to enter the kingdom of God.' " He had come to an awareness that earthly riches promise to satisfy, but they simply can't. It was a transforming moment in this man's life. From that day on, he saw everything he had as a gift from God, and everything in his life changed.

We need to realize that money isn't evil; it's the love of money that Paul calls "the root of all evil." When we treasure money and stuff more than Jesus Christ, we make those things an idol in our hearts. If God has given you wealth, you don't need to feel guilty, but watch out for pride! Recognize that you are a steward who will give an account, enjoy God's blessings, and be generous to share with those in need.

As we build our perspective about money and giving on the firm foundation of God's grace, we need to ask two questions: "How should we give?" And, "How much should we give?" Let's take a look at those questions.

> **Recognize that you are a steward who will give an account, enjoy God's blessings, and be generous to share with those in need.**

HOW SHOULD WE GIVE?

As we experience the grace of God, our hearts will want to express our gratitude by giving generously, cheerfully, and expectantly.

Give generously.

We'll get to the specifics later in the chapter, but for now, we note that Paul instructed people, "Remember this: Whoever sows sparingly will also reap sparingly, and whoever sows generously will also reap generously" (9:6).

I believe most of us know when we are being generous . . . and when we're not. When I'm generous, I have a sense of anticipation that I'm doing something that taps into the heart of God. I get a rush, a thrill. I can't wait to see how God uses my gift to transform lives! That leads us to the second characteristic.

Give cheerfully.

In the most quoted verse in these chapters, Paul reminds us, "Each man should give what he has decided in his heart to give, not reluctantly or under compulsion, for God loves a cheerful giver" (9:7). Maybe you've heard the old saying, "Give 'til it hurts." A member of our church told me, "Don't give 'til it hurts. Give 'til it feels good!" The Greek word Paul uses is hilaron, from which we get the word "hilarious." That's God's desire for each of us, that we would be so thrilled to partner with him that we'd laugh out loud when we put a check in the offering plate!

A few years ago, a lady tried to justify her meager contributions by telling me, "Remember, Pastor K, God loves a *cheerful* giver."

I replied, "Yes, but also remember that God loves a cheerful *giver.*"

Don't let anybody—pastor, teacher, friend, family member, or Satan—pressure you to give. If you are reluctant to open your hand and give with great joy, go back and consider again the vast wealth of grace that God has poured out on you. (That's the best remedy for stinginess I've ever seen.) And then decide what you will be thrilled to give, and give it with your whole heart.

> That's God's desire for each of us, that we would be so thrilled to partner with him that we'd laugh out loud when we put a check in the offering plate!

Give expectantly.

Jesus assured his followers of the principle of sowing and reaping when he promised, "Give, and it will be given to you. A good measure, pressed down, shaken together and running over, will be poured into your lap. For with the measure you use, it will be measured to you" (Luke 6:38).

Paul explains that we can be sure that God will bless those we give to and us as well. He told the Corinthians, "And God is able to make all grace abound to you, so that in all things at all times, having all that you need, you will abound in every good work. As it is written:

'He has scattered abroad his gifts to the poor;
   his righteousness endures forever.'
Now he who supplies seed to the sower and bread for food
will also supply and increase your store of seed and will enlarge
the harvest of your righteousness" (9:8-10).

Could Jesus or Paul be any clearer? I don't think so. We can
expect God to fulfill the promise inherent in the principle of
sowing and reaping, but be careful. I'll be honest with you: Some
of the television preachers drive me nuts! God isn't a vending
machine. He's not a slot machine either! We don't pop in some
cash and get out more than we put in. I don't give in order to get
more. I give because I've already gotten so much from God and
I'm thankful.

God's main interest isn't our wealth—it's our faith. He wants
to develop our trust in him, and sometimes, he temporarily sus-
pends the law of sowing and reaping to test us and refocus our
hearts on him. Some of the most consistently generous people
I know have had setbacks in business from time to time. If they
had become resentful because God didn't protect their businesses
during a recession or some other economic downturn, they would
have missed some of the greatest lessons of their lives. During
those times, they had to reassess their finances, but they kept their
hearts riveted on the grace of God, and they trusted God to provide
for them. Quite often, God provides far more than we need, but
sometimes he gives us only what we need. Either way, Paul reminds
us, we can be content because we trust in him.

> **God's main interest isn't our wealth—it's our faith.**

As a general principle, though, God has promised to bless
us as we trust him by giving to him and his cause. In fact, God
invites us to test him to prove his promise is true. God spoke
through the prophet Malachi: " 'Bring the whole tithe into the
storehouse, that there may be food in my house. Test me in this,'

says the LORD Almighty, 'and see if I will not throw open the floodgates of heaven and pour out so much blessing that you will not have room enough for it. I will prevent pests from devouring your crops, and the vines in your fields will not cast their fruit,' says the LORD Almighty. 'Then all the nations will call you blessed, for yours will be a delightful land,' says the LORD Almighty" (Malachi 3:10-12). Nowhere else in Scripture are we told to "test" God's faithfulness, but I believe that, because our finances are so close to our hearts, God invites us to test him in this area of our lives. And he'll prove himself to be faithful. You can count on it.

HOW MUCH SHOULD WE GIVE?

I was shocked when I read the report of a survey about giving by American Christians. The study revealed that poorer Americans give a greater percentage of their income to charity than those with far greater wealth. In 1998, those who earned under $20,000 gave 5.1%, those who earned $10,000 to $19,900 gave 3.3%, and those who earned $75,000 to $99,999 gave only 1.6%. As I read these statistics, I felt Jesus' words burn in my heart: "To whom much is given, much is required."

We talk often about "tithes," "offerings," "gifts," and other "contributions" to the church and other organizations. Let me provide some background and context for our analysis of how much we should give.

The Old Testament provides insights and instructions about giving. We read in Genesis 14 that Abraham gave ten percent, a tithe, of his spoils of battle to Melchizedek, who was the priest of the Most High God. Interestingly, Abraham's offering was given before the law prescribed that gifts to God should be a tenth.

Years later, Moses came down from the mountain in Sinai with the Ten Commandments. During this time, God instructed his people to give several types of offerings, including:

- The Levites' tithe, outlined in Leviticus 27:30, says that people were to give ten percent to the priests for their ministry.

This offering covered everything that was produced: grain, wine, livestock, and all. God himself branded those who refused to give as thieves. In Malachi 3:8, God warns, "Will a man rob God? Yet you rob me. You ask, 'How do we rob you?' In tithes and offerings."

- The festival tithe, described in Deuteronomy 12:10-11, was the gift of a tenth of their income and was to be used for celebrations to commemorate God's gracious provisions. Combined with the Levite's tithe, the total for these two was 20 percent.

- The poor tithe, stated in Deuteronomy 14:28-29, was designed to provide for those who couldn't provide for themselves: aliens, widows, orphans, crippled people, and the poor. This gift of ten percent was given every three years.

- Profit-sharing with the poor, described in Leviticus 19:9-10, instructs people to leave part of their harvest in the field for poor people to harvest for their needs. This was the work Ruth was doing after her husband died and she desperately needed food to survive.

- The temple charge was a third of a shekel and was required as payment for materials for worship in the temple.

So far, the people of Israel were required to give about 25 percent of their income. But there's more . . .

- First fruits were given from the first portion of the harvest each year, and the farmer trusted that God would bless the rest of his crop. This was a voluntary offering to God.

- Free-will offerings were given for special projects, such as building the Temple.

The total for any family under the Old Covenant was about 30 percent of their income. That sends shockwaves through most of us, but God's people were reminded again and again that giving was an opportunity to participate in God's work on earth.

Under the New Covenant, however, God doesn't get 30 percent. He gets it all. That's right. All of it is his. We are simply stewards of the part he has entrusted to us. In Matthew's account of the life of Christ, Jesus affirmed the tithe as a benchmark for giving (see Matthew 23:23), but it's a minimum, not a maximum for us. The tithe isn't a law for New Testament believers like us. It's simply a good starting point.

> **Under the New Covenant, however, God doesn't get 30 percent. He gets it all.**

SOME STEPS TO TAKE

Let me offer a few suggestions to help you respond to the grace of God in your life so you can give more generously, cheerfully, and expectantly:

Start where you are.

You may look at your finances and think, "Man, I'm in debt up to my eyeballs! Will the church take a credit card? No, that won't work. I want to give, but I sure can't find ten percent to give right now." The first and most important step is to reflect deeply and often on the grace principles in this chapter and this book. As your heart overflows with love for God, you'll want to express your devotion in every way possible. One of those ways is through being a good steward of the resources God has entrusted to you. You'll want to get out of debt and use your money wisely, like giving to Christ's cause. Paul told the Corinthians, "For if the willingness is there, the gift is acceptable according to what one has, not according to what he does not have" (8:12).

No matter what your finances look like, give some now, as much as you can, and as you get your life in order, raise the level of your giving. That's an application of repentance: confession, forgiveness, and amendment.

Focus on how much you've received from God.

You and I are incredibly wealthy. "Well, no," some of us might be tempted to say, "I don't have a new boat like Frank, or a new car like Janice, or a big house like the Marshalls." If we compare ourselves with the next level (or two or three levels) up the economic ladder, we'll always feel disappointed and sorry for ourselves. But if we focus on what we actually deserve—eternal condemnation—then we realize we are rich beyond measure! That's in the spiritual realm. On a more practical, tangible level, middle-class Americans enjoy a standard of living that would be the envy of the wealthiest people in the world only a couple of generations ago, and the envy of most of the world today. If you're going to compare, look through eyes of gratitude and truth, not envy and demands.

Ask God for wisdom and direction.

Giving is one of the most spiritual things I do, and I want God's involvement in my financial decisions. I regularly ask him to lead me in every part of money management. Sometimes, God makes me aware of special needs so I can help meet them. That's in addition to the regular discipline of giving Elaine and I have established.

Like every other part of my Christian walk, I have ups and downs in my motivation to give. Usually, I am thrilled to give money to the Lord's cause, but at other times, I don't feel all that excited. I just give because it's a commitment and a discipline, and that's just fine for me, for Elaine, and for Christ. I don't think he died on the cross with a smile on his face, and I'm pretty sure he understands that sometimes we obey without a lot of warm, wonderful feelings. That's just part of our walk of faith.

Realize you will give an account one day.

As stewards of part of what God owns, you and I will someday stand before him to receive a report card of our care for his possessions. You and I are rich, so Paul's advice to Timothy applies to us. He wrote, "Command those who are rich in this present world not to be arrogant nor to put their hope in wealth, which is so uncertain, but to put their hope in God, who richly provides us with everything for our enjoyment. Command them to do good, to be rich in good deeds, and to be generous and willing to share. In this way they will lay up treasure for themselves as a firm foundation for the coming age, so that they may take hold of the life that is truly life" (1 Timothy 6:17-19).

Paul echoed Jesus' encouragement to "store up for yourselves treasures in heaven, where moth and rust do not destroy, and where thieves do not break in and steal. For where your treasure is, there your heart will be also" (Matthew 6:20).

You may have a million excuses for not giving, but you can be sure that God is loving and fair. When we have plenty, we can help those in need. We saw this principle in action after the hurricanes, and we see it all the time in less conspicuous ways. Paul wrote, "Our desire is not that others might be relieved while you are hard pressed, but that there might be equality. At the present time your plenty will supply what they need, so that in turn their plenty will supply what you need. Then there will be equality, as it is written: 'He who gathered much did not have too much, and he who gathered little did not have too little' " (2 Corinthians 8:13-15).

Watch what you buy.

The statistics about personal debt in our society are staggering. Many Christians worry in their waking hours (and toss and turn in their sleep) because they are so far in debt. If that's your case, find a reputable credit counselor, go to a debt-free seminar, read a book, listen to CDs, and do whatever it takes for you to be free from the crushing load of debt. Some of us experience unforeseen expenses, but many others slip into the bad habit of regularly spending beyond their means.

To get out of debt, you'll have to make some hard decisions to change your lifestyle and buying habits. But when you are free from the burden of debt, you will feel so much better

> **But when you are free from the burden of debt, you will feel so much better about yourself, and you'll be able to respond far more easily to the Spirit's prompting to live, serve, and give with your whole heart.**

about yourself, and you'll be able to respond far more easily to the Spirit's prompting to live, serve, and give with your whole heart.

Learn to manage your wealth.

I understand that most Americans own stocks or mutual funds. As wise stewards of all God has given us, we need to take our responsibility seriously and learn to manage our wealth wisely. Our church offers a money management class, and people have learned valuable principles. Most class members have reduced their credit card debt by thousands of dollars during the course of the study.

John Wesley, the founder of the Methodist movement, advised, "Earn all you can, save all you can, and give all you can." That's good advice for us, too.

Give more each year.

I learned to give by watching my parents. They never made a big deal of their generosity. They just gave, and I watched them give cheerfully and expectantly. Watching them taught me to tithe, but I learned to give beyond the tithe because a man visiting my first church, Gene Friesen, asked me a penetrating question: "Pastor, are you growing in your giving?"

I replied, "I'm giving more this year than last year."

"That's good," Gene replied, "but that's not exactly what I meant. Are you giving a larger percentage than before?"

I answered, "No, I still give ten percent."

He told me about the commitment he and his wife had made. "Seven years ago, we decided to give a half a percent more each year than the year before. This year, we are giving thirteen and a half percent of our income, and thirteen years from now, we plan to be at twenty percent."

I almost fell off my chair. (By the way, Gene spent his years in a wheelchair.)

Elaine and I have tried to raise our level of giving each year, too. I recommend that people consider giving one-half or one percent more each year. Don't compare your gift to someone who gives more than you. Start where you are, and if you're married, make a commitment to God, with your spouse, that you want to trust him by giving a little higher portion of your income to him each year. Then stand back and see what happens!

Make a written commitment.

A written commitment is obviously a major help to the leaders of our church as we develop our budget each year. We develop our budget based on the promises of our members and other anticipated gifts. A written commitment is also helpful to the person who makes it. A friend, who is a pastor, knew the importance of making a commitment in advance (as the Corinthian Christians did). He told his congregation, "If you pray about and write down your commitment once in the fall, you don't have to wrestle the devil 52 times next year!" I agree with him 100 percent. At Gloria Dei, our members receive a letter from me encouraging them to make their commitment, and with the letter, we include an appropriate number of commitment cards and privacy envelopes. We will remind them of the principles of "grace giving" to help them grow as generous stewards of the gifts of God.

> **Then stand back and see what happens!**

Follow through.

All the encouragement, examples, background, and principles in the world only prepare us to act. We need to follow through with our commitments. Paul understood that fact, so he wrote, "And here is my advice about what is best for you in this matter: Last year you were the first not only to give but also to have the desire to do so. Now finish the work, so that your eager willingness to do it may be matched by your completion of it, according to your means" (2 Corinthians 8:10-11).

Let me warn you: You can have all kinds of pleasant feelings about God, but when you take out your pen and checkbook, the devil will try to stop you in your tracks. You'll think about how much you really want that new plasma-screen television, and if you just skip this month's offering (and maybe next month's), you can get it. Or you'll be mad at your spouse and forget to write the check. Or you'll think, "You know, the message (or the music or whatever) last week wasn't that good. I think I won't send in my offering this time because they don't deserve it." Or maybe you'll be a really good Lutheran and wonder, "I'm not completely sure I'm as cheerful about this gift as I should be. I really feel bad for not being cheerful enough. I'm a terrible person. In fact, God won't even want me to give because I'm so bad!" Recognize the enemy's schemes to get you off track, and fight against him with truth and obedience.

Leaders need to set a good example for others to follow. In the early 1990's we decided to move from a Church Council structure to a Board of Directors model. In the first meeting of our new Board we talked about our expectations of one another as board members. Tina Heinbaugh, a young mother and wife in her early 30's, and a wonderful Christian woman, very matter-of-factly announced, "I expect everybody around this table to tithe to this church. If we can't manage our own households' finances, we're not qualified to manage the

> **Recognize the enemy's schemes to get you off track, and fight against him with truth and obedience.**

finances of the household of God." Her insight and commitment touched me and the other board members deeply.

Give something special from time to time.

I know some people who have developed the discipline of giving regularly, but from time to time they delight in giving something bigger and better. One man gives big chunks of money to people in need, and about once a year, the Holy Spirit prompts a lady to give away something (a piece of art, a cherished dish, a fine dress) to a needy person. Their delight is multiplied because, if it's possible, they give these gifts anonymously.

RECIPIENTS

We experience the joy of giving by taking the risk to give. Like every other area of our spiritual lives, Christians live under grace. People don't go to hell if they don't tithe, just as they don't go to hell if they don't pray or read the Bible as much as they could. But they miss out on so much when they don't follow Jesus and pursue him with their whole hearts. Fear cripples us by convincing us that we don't want to entrust our lives to another person, even if that person is our provider, redeemer, and sustainer. But real life is lived on the edge of excitement as we muster the courage to put our hands into God's hand and say, "OK, I'm ready. Let's go!" The first steps may be small, but they are crucial in developing healthy disciplines.

In this chapter, we began by being refreshed by the grace of God toward us. He has given us forgiveness, eternal life, rich relationships with him and the family of God, and riches beyond measure. We then looked at our response to the grace of God, that we are his stewards who delight in storing up treasures in heaven by making good decisions with the money he has entrusted to us. At the end of Paul's encouragement to the Corinthians, he praises them for their faithfulness. He wrote, "Because of the service by which you have proved yourselves, men will praise God for the obedience that accompanies your confession of the gospel of Christ, and for your generosity in sharing with them and with everyone else. And in their prayers for you their hearts will go out to you, because of the surpassing grace God has given you" (9:13-14).

Paul closes with a flourish, reminding them again that they have received the greatest gift anyone could ever imagine, Jesus Christ. He exclaims, "Thanks be to God for his indescribable gift!" (9:15).

God wants us to excel in every area of our lives—"in faith, in speech, in knowledge, in complete earnestness and in your love for us." I hope that we all commit ourselves to also "excel in this grace of giving" in response to God's gift to us. Regardless of our past experiences in giving, believe this: The best is yet to come!

THINK ABOUT IT

1. Read 2 Corinthians 8:1-9 and paraphrase these verses. Why is the concept of grace in verse 9 so crucial to a lifestyle of cheerful and generous giving?

2. Before you read this chapter, what was your motivation for giving? What barriers (doubt, debt, demands, etc.) did you experience along the way? After reading Chapter 8, what motivates you most now?

3. Describe what it means to give generously, cheerfully, and expectantly.

4. Review the steps at the end of the chapter. Which one(s) do you need to take? Write a plan for the action you need to take to implement these steps.

GOING DEEPER

1. Read Psalm 50:7-12. What would it mean in your life if you were completely convinced that God owns everything and you are his steward?

2. Describe a time in your life when you gave away something important to you and loved giving it.

3. Is your level of debt cramping your ability to serve and give as generously as you feel is right? If so, what specific steps can you take to be free of that debt? If not, what decisions did you and your family make early in your lives that have kept you free from this burden?

9 · Growth
WALKING THROUGH THE DOORS

"Let us fix our eyes on Jesus, the author and perfecter of our faith, who for the joy set before him endured the cross, scorning its shame, and sat down at the right hand of the throne of God. Consider him who endured such opposition from sinful men, so that you will not grow weary and lose heart" (Hebrews 12:2-3).

"Whatever faith may be, and whatever answers it may give, and to whomsoever it gives them, every such answer gives to the finite existence of man an infinite meaning, a meaning not destroyed by suffering, deprivations, or death." —Leo Tolstoy

Over the years, God has given me the privilege of seeing him at work in the lives of thousands of people. But during that time, I've also seen the tragedy of lives shattered by stupid choices. In some ways, growth is a mystery, but in others, it's simply the product of sowing good decisions and reaping rich rewards of spiritual fruit. We all face ups and downs in life, but our perspective on both makes all the difference. Good times can produce gratitude, but they also can lead people astray as they become complacent about their need for God. Difficulties can discourage people so much that they give up, but suffering can show us our genuine need for God's direction and care.

To grow in our faith, we need to build a firm foundation of trust and truth. When we center our lives on Jesus Christ and respond to his invitation to walk through the doors of the disciplines, we grow in our commitment to him and his cause.

BUILDING ON THE ROCK

What or who do you trust in? What or who gives your life meaning? What or who do you run to in times of celebration? What or who do you look for when you are in trouble? The answer to those questions (don't answer them too quickly!) identifies the foundation of our lives. And that foundation might be solid or shaky.

At the end of his most famous sermon, Jesus told a story about two men who built houses. He said, "Therefore everyone who hears these words of mine and puts them into practice is like a wise man who built his house on the rock. The rain came down, the streams rose, and the winds blew and beat against that house; yet it did not fall, because it had its foundation on the rock. But everyone who hears these words of mine and does not put them into practice is like a foolish man who built his house on sand. The rain came down, the streams rose, and the winds blew and beat against that house, and it fell with a great crash" (Matthew 7:24-27).

Two men, two houses, two foundations, two different results. I enjoy watching workmen build houses, and in our community, we get plenty of chances to see them at work. The process is long and hard, involving many people and many steps. The workmen prepare the soil and build the frame for the foundation, pour the concrete, frame the house, install all the wiring and plumbing, apply the brick or wood to the façade, sheet rock the rooms, put on the roof, and finish every facet of the construction. (I'm sure I left out some steps, but you get the picture.) In our area, though, the foundation is not always as stable as it looks when the new owner walks in the door. Clay soils shift in the floods and droughts, and many houses suffer cracked foundations.

When prospective buyers talk to builders in this area, the builders usually tell them what they've done to stabilize the soil and build a stable foundation. It may sound boring, but it's essential information. That's the message Jesus is giving us at the end of his sermon. A wise man pays close attention to the base for the foundation, an element that often isn't noticed, but makes all the difference in the strength of the house. A foolish builder, though, chooses (or fails to notice and avoid) ground that is shifting sand.

The rock of our lives is Jesus Christ. Not religion, not church, not spirituality, not philosophy, not good feelings about God, and certainly not any list of rules we might try to follow to earn God's acceptance. No, the rock is Jesus Christ himself. I want to make this point at the beginning of the chapter on growth because it's so easy for us to shift our eyes, ever so slightly, to techniques of growth or measurements of growth instead of the only one who is worthy of our affection and attention. At least, it's easy for me to shift my focus to those things I can control, those things I can see, and those things I can show to others to prove I'm a really good Christian. But Jesus isn't too interested with those things. He's only interested in me when I am fully devoted and committed to him alone.

> **At least, it's easy for me to shift my focus to those things I can control, those things I can see, and those things I can show to others to prove I'm a really good Christian.**

Lives don't change just by understanding principles, even biblical principles. We have to *act* on them. We must be committed to them. Some people don't act on the encouragements of this book because they feel ashamed, and they can't imagine God could really love them. Some are complacent and think, "Oh, I already know all this stuff. I don't need to do anything with it." And some secretly harbor sins they cherish far more than the forgiveness and hope God offers them. Many feel lonely and afraid, and they need someone to pat them on the shoulder and tell them, "Come with me. Let's learn to walk with God together." For any number of reasons, we can remain stuck until and unless we find a sense of hope that the best really is yet to come.

EVERYBODY, EVEN YOU AND ME

I've talked to scores, maybe hundreds, of people who come to church, but when we chat about walking with God, they mumble, shift their feet, and make excuses. If they stay engaged in the conversation with me, I often learn that they feel ashamed of themselves, and they just can't imagine that God would *tolerate* them, much less *treasure* them, and they certainly can't fathom the idea that God wants to partner with them in the greatest adventure the world has ever known! But he does. And it's all about grace.

Some of us are addicted to drugs, alcohol, sex, gambling, food, or some other substance or activity. And living with an addict has devastated others among us. Some are depressed, some experience mental illness, and some have been crushed by grief. Some of us have been victimized, and some are perpetrators. Some are furious, and some are so numb they're almost unconscious. All of us, though, can experience the cleansing and power of Christ's death to pay for our sins and his resurrection that gives us hope and strength.

God doesn't excuse our sins. He doesn't say, "Oh, that's OK. It doesn't matter what you've done. I don't care." No, he cares very much. Our sins separate us from him, and that's why Christ came. But our sins don't ultimately disqualify us from experiencing the presence and power of God. Paul wrote the Corinthians that every person on earth could experience God's grace: "Do you not know that the wicked will not inherit the kingdom of God? Do not be deceived: Neither the sexually immoral nor idolaters nor adulterers nor male prostitutes nor homosexual offenders nor thieves nor the greedy nor drunkards nor slanderers nor swindlers will inherit the kingdom of God. And that is what some of you were. But you were washed, you were sanctified, you were justified in the name of the Lord Jesus Christ and by the Spirit of our God" (1 Corinthians 6:9-11).

Do you see it? No matter what we've done or who we are, God washes us clean, and declares us right with him because of Christ's payment for our sin. He then sanctifies us by transforming us slowly into the likeness and image of his son. There's only one qualification for experiencing grace: honesty about the need for forgiveness. Do you and I qualify?

In one of the most poignant stories in the gospels, Jesus was invited to the home of Simon, a respected Pharisee. When he walked in, Simon didn't give him the customary greeting offered to guests in a home: washing his feet, giving him a welcoming kiss on the cheek, and pouring a little oil on his head. As they ate their dinner, a woman barged in, unannounced and unwelcome by Simon. She had been touched by God's forgiveness. She immediately fell at Jesus' feet, poured out an alabaster jar of perfume, and bathed his feet with her tears and hair, kissing and pouring the perfume on them.

> There's only one qualification for experiencing grace: honesty about the need for forgiveness. Do you and I qualify?

Simon was horrified that such a despicable person would intrude into his private dinner and carry on like that! But Jesus looked at her and recounted the fact that she had done in love what Simon wouldn't even do in common courtesy. I have to ask myself: Am I more like Simon or the woman? Do I sit back and analyze Christ and Christians and withhold affection from them, or am I so grateful for his grace toward me that nothing can hold me back from expressing my affection?

The woman was a social outcast, much like an addict, an unwed mother, or a person with a bad reputation for any reason, but she recognized her need for grace and went away with the experience of loving and being loved by Jesus. His grace is for everybody . . . including you and me.

David's beautiful and heartfelt message in Psalm 51 expresses the desire of every one of us who has fallen short of God's desires—and that includes all of us. He confesses his sins without excusing himself or blaming anyone else, and he trusts in God's great grace to forgive him. He prays,

"Create in me a pure heart, O God,
  and renew a steadfast spirit within me.
Restore to me the joy of your salvation
  and grant me a willing spirit, to sustain me"
  (Psalm 51:10, 12).

Only in God's forgiveness, David was sure, could he find new meaning and purpose in life. He writes,

"Then I will teach transgressors your ways,
  and sinners will turn back to you.
Save me from bloodguilt, O God,
  the God who saves me,
  and my tongue will sing of your righteousness.
O Lord, open my lips,
  and my mouth will declare your praise" (51:13-15).

David was assured that God delighted in his honesty, his confession, and his experience of God's grace. He prayed,

"The sacrifices of God are a broken spirit;
  a broken and contrite heart,
  O God, you will not despise" (51:17).

We can have that same assurance of God's forgiveness. The steadfast love of the Lord never fails. It is new every morning, and that fact gives me hope and strength to follow him.

STAGES OF GROWTH

Author Philip Yancey identifies the stages of spiritual growth as *child, adult,* and *parent.*[25] In our spiritual infancy and childhood, we need a lot of care. We make a lot of mistakes, so we need to be in relationships with people who will encourage us a lot, and correct us when we need it—which is fairly often! In this stage, we use trial and error to see how life works, and we learn as much from the results of our errors as we do from our successes. Yancey comments that much of the Bible seems to be written for people in the "child" stage because there are so many clear, simple commands, just like those a parent gives a child. In this stage, we experiment with the doors of spiritual disciplines. Failures and successes mark our progress, but we learn how to practice the disciplines in meaningful ways.

As the child grows into adulthood, values are internalized and disciplines are established. As a spiritual "adult," the person has a sense of purpose. When we are baby Christians, everything is about us: *my* growth, *my* happiness, and God giving *me* what I want. But as an adult, we care more for God's purposes and his work to redeem people. We identify our skills and find roles that fit us. The spiritual disciplines become a vital part of our walks with Christ, and we use them to know him better. We grow in our depth of biblical knowledge and are able to chew some spiritual meat from the Scriptures. In the adult stage, we enjoy strong, healthy relationships with others because we are able to give and receive. We aren't focused on meeting our childish, selfish needs all the time.

> In this stage, we experiment with the doors of spiritual disciplines. Failures and successes mark our progress, but we learn how to practice the disciplines in meaningful ways.

As we continue to grow, God puts us in a leadership role, like a parent. We become trusted friends to others who are growing in their faith, and they look to us for wisdom, perspective, and hope. In this way, we perform the role of a parent in their lives as we help them grow up spiritually. In this stage, we teach others how to practice the spiritual disciplines in ways that fit their personalities, experiences, and needs.

Through all of these stages, we need friends who are partners with us in the adventure of walking with Christ. Paul invited people to follow him as he followed Christ. He told the Philippians, "Whatever you have learned or received or heard from me, or seen in me—put it into practice. And the God of peace will be with you" (Philippians 4:9).

Don't try to walk with God alone. He wants each of us to find rich, encouraging relationships in the family of God. Look for a small group, a support group, a class, or a trusted friend, so you can develop wonderful friendships. The encouragement, accountability, and fun you'll find will stimulate your growth . . . and theirs, too.

A group of Christians in the child stage is like a room full of toddlers, often experiencing conflicts and misunderstandings. But as we mature, our skills in relationships enable us to enjoy adult-adult relationships with other believers. In that environment, trust grows, we become more vulnerable, and we are able to share even more of our hopes and hurts with those who have earned our trust. But even in the parent stage, we haven't arrived. In his letter to the Philippians, Paul disclosed, "Not that I have already obtained all this, or have already been made perfect, but I press on to take hold of that for which Christ Jesus took hold of me. Brothers, I do not consider myself yet to have taken hold of it. But one thing I do: Forgetting what is behind and straining toward what is ahead, I press on toward the goal to win the prize for which God has called me heavenward in Christ Jesus" (Philippians 3:12-14). If Paul didn't think he had arrived, then I sure haven't either!

BEHIND EVERY DOOR

As we grow, we learn to look for Jesus behind every door of opportunity and challenge in our lives. His invitation summons us to participate in each of the disciplines, and every encounter with people and circumstance invites us to trust him for wisdom and strength.

The role of the Holy Spirit is one that many Christians have neglected, but as we grow, we learn that the Spirit of God plays a vital role in our lives. It is his voice that whispers to us to turn in one direction or another—or, in my case, to stop! His power gives us the courage to take bold steps, and his comfort soothes our hearts when they hurt.

The disciplines aren't steps that guarantee spiritual growth. Instead, they are doors of growth which lead us into the presence of God. We don't "perform" them to earn points to show how godly we are. We use them "to know the love of Christ which surpasses knowledge." To be sure, practicing these disciplines can be tedious, so we need to remember to look for Christ when we participate in them. In my own life, I find Jesus behind the doors of prayer, Bible study, witness, and the others. That's always a thrill, but he's there whether I sense him or not. In that, I can be confident.

> **The disciplines aren't steps that guarantee spiritual growth. Instead, they are doors of growth which lead us into the presence of God.**

And knowing that he's there makes life both a mystery and an adventure. I can't forget that the one who's behind every door is the infinite God, the creator of heaven and earth, the one who spoke—and a magnificent universe was born. He's the same one who has called me—me!—in Jesus Christ to be his partner in touching people's lives. And he's the same one who is calling you, too.

THE HARD ROAD

Difficult times in our lives force us to go in one direction or the other. Tears and anger don't allow us to stay still. In my years of helping people grow in their faith, God has used difficulties more than anything else as fertile soil for growth. I wish that weren't true, but it is.

When childish Christians live in a self-absorbed culture, they can expect difficulties to shock them. The most common question I hear when people suffer is, "Why me?" The answer to that question is as varied as the situations. It could be dumb personal choices, the sins of others, disease, natural disasters, or a host of other reasons, but ultimately, the right question needs to be asked. That question is, "What do you have for me in this, Lord? I'm listening."

God may want us to change direction in our lives, and he may use a calamity to get our attention. Or he may want us to repent of a sin, and the difficulty prompts reflection and the conviction that we have been wrong. Or perhaps a disease shows us our mortality, and we come face to face with the reality of eternity. And sometimes, the trauma simply makes no sense at all. In any and every troubled situation, God longs for us to look to him, cling to him, and depend on him. In the 18th century, Jean-Pierre de Caussade wrote poignantly, "A living faith is nothing else than a steadfast pursuit of God through all that disguises, disfigures, demolishes and seeks, so to speak, to abolish him. Love and accept the present moment as the best, with perfect trust in God's universal goodness. . . . Everything without exception is an instrument and means of sanctification. . . . God's purpose for us is always what will contribute most to our good."[26]

Times of pain, disappointment, pruning, and waiting on God's answers to our prayers are parts of God's plan to deepen our trust in him. We naturally try to avoid pain, but if we push it away, we may miss God's purpose for it. In his insightful book, *Knowing God*, J. I. Packer observed that God has a higher purpose than helping us avoid pain. He wrote, "This is what all the work of grace aims at—an even deeper knowledge of God, and an ever closer

> **We naturally try to avoid pain, but if we push it away, we may miss God's purpose for it.**

fellowship with Him. Grace is God drawing us sinners closer and closer to Him. How does God in grace prosecute this purpose? Not by shielding us from assault by the world, the flesh, and the devil, nor by protecting us from burdensome and frustrating circumstances, nor yet by shielding us from troubles created by our own temperament and psychology; but rather by exposing us to all these things, so as to overwhelm us with a sense of our own inadequacy, and to drive us to cling to Him more closely. This is the ultimate reason, from our standpoint, why God fills our lives with troubles and perplexities of one sort or another—it is to ensure that we shall learn to hold Him fast."[27]

Should we pray for healing and relief from suffering? Absolutely! God sometimes works miracles. But we need to be prepared for him to say "No." Paul experienced a lingering pain that he called a "thorn in the flesh." It was so severe that he prayed three times for God to take it away. God then spoke to Paul and assured him, "My grace is sufficient for you, for my power is made perfect in weakness" (2 Corinthians 12:9a). Was Paul angry with God when he heard this answer? No, far from it. He was satisfied in the core of his being with the grace of God. His response was exactly the opposite of self-pity and anger. He wrote, "Therefore I will boast all the more gladly about my weaknesses, so that Christ's power may rest on me. That is why, for Christ's sake, I delight in weaknesses, in insults, in hardships, in persecution, in difficulties. For when I am weak, then I am strong" (12:9b-10). Wow! Delighting in weakness. What a concept! How could he have this kind of attitude? Because he lived completely "for Christ's sake," not for comfort, approval, or riches. And that makes all the difference.

It's a strange life, isn't it? We enjoy the love and blessings of God, but we still long for Eden, where there's no pain, only joy. We live today in the "in between," squarely in the middle of the "already" and the "not yet." As we grasp that fact and trust in God's goodness and purpose, even when we can't fathom what's going on, our faith in him will continue to grow. It won't be easy, but it's worth it.

REMINDERS OF GRACE

One of the clearest descriptions of spiritual growth in the Bible is in Peter's second letter. In the first chapter, he outlines the stages of growth, from the first step, "giving up the gross stuff," to the ultimate stage, the ability to express unconditional agape love. He wrote, "For this very reason, make every effort to add to your faith goodness; and to goodness, knowledge; and to knowledge, self-control; and to self-control, perseverance; and to perseverance, godliness; and to godliness, brotherly kindness; and to brotherly kindness, love" (2 Peter 1:5-7).

How does this growth occur? By grace, through commitment. Peter tells us, "For if you possess these qualities in increasing measure, they will keep you from being ineffective and unproductive in your knowledge of our Lord Jesus Christ. But if anyone does not have them, he is nearsighted and blind, and has forgotten that he has been cleansed from his past sins" (1:8-9). Spiritual growth, Peter says, is blocked when we lose sight of Christ's forgiveness. At any point in our Christian walks, we can forget the focal point, the foundation of our lives, which is the forgiveness we received by the grace of God through Christ. But if we keep our eyes on him, the source of truth, the power of his Spirit, and the gift of encouragement will enable us to keep growing strong.

> **Spiritual growth, Peter says, is blocked when we lose sight of Christ's forgiveness.**

In these pages, we've mentioned the necessity of a heart of repentance. That's Peter's message in this passage, too. If we forget grace, we become stiff, hardhearted, and condemning of others, just like the Pharisees. Even a glance at the gospels shows us that Jesus reserved his harshest criticisms for them. Why? Because they were the leaders of the nation, and their lack of grace was leading people astray, and indeed, crushing them spiritually.

Today, I'm more mindful than ever that I, like Paul, am "the chief of sinners." Some people would hear me and say, "Oh, Pastor K, you aren't that bad. Lighten up!" But these people don't know the dark recesses of my heart. They don't know that only the grace of God keeps me from being thoroughly selfish and bitter. They don't know how much I desperately need God's forgiveness and strength, all day, every day. But Peter knew. And God knows. And I have a pretty good hunch myself.

Acts of repentance aren't just for believers in the child stage. Confession, absolution, and amendment are for all of us, all day, every day. Certainly, the sins we confess at the beginning of our Christian experience can be "the gross stuff," but as we mature, the Holy Spirit reveals sins that have lain hidden for years and are just now coming to light. We realize we have harbored jealousy, envy, and resentment, not only of outsiders, but also of our brothers and sisters in Christ! And we've failed—and failed miserably—to "love one another" as Christ loves us: completely, sacrificially, passionately, and selflessly. No, I need to practice the disciplines of grace in my life as much as I need to breathe, eat, and sleep . . . maybe more. Repentance provides the cleansing, refreshment, and refocus I need to keep my eyes on Jesus.

> **No, I need to practice the disciplines of grace in my life as much as I need to breathe, eat, and sleep . . . maybe more. Repentance provides the cleansing, refreshment, and refocus I need to keep my eyes on Jesus.**

INTENTIONAL AND MYSTERIOUS

As I read books and listen to Christian speakers, I'm sometimes amazed with the passivity I hear them suggest. Some of them say things that sound very spiritual, like, "We just need to

get out of the way and let God work," or "I'm going to stop trying and start trusting." From these comments, it sounds like our
efforts are never appropriate, so we should just remain passive
and let God work alone. But that's not the message I read in
the Scriptures. Certainly, we are to trust God for wisdom and
strength, but we are partners in the enterprise, with responsibility to take action. When Paul told the Colossian believers about
his goal of reaching every person with the transforming gospel
of Christ, he explained, "To this end I labor, struggling with all
his energy, which so powerfully works in me" (Colossians 1:29).
This verse and many others like it explain the dynamic nature
of the partnership. We labor and struggle, trusting in him and
drawing on his energy to accomplish his purposes. We are active
and intentional.

Spiritual growth occurs when we make commitments and
take action, but the working of God in the human heart is mysterious. We aren't machines that can be programmed to respond
the same way each time or the same as every other machine.
Jesus told a parable to illustrate the mysterious nature of spiritual growth. He told his followers, "This is what the kingdom of
God is like. A man scatters seed on the ground. Night and day,
whether he sleeps or gets up, the seed sprouts and grows, though
he does not know how. All by itself the soil produces grain—first
the stalk, then the head, then the full kernel in the head. As soon
as the grain is ripe, he puts the sickle to it, because the harvest
has come" (Mark 4:26-29).

Spiritual growth, Jesus was saying, is mysterious, and it is also
gradual. A person doesn't become mature overnight. Natural
processes of plant growth include fertile soil, water, sun, fertil-
izer, weeding, and time. In the spiritual realm, a person learns
to use seven disciplines to know Christ and respond to him in
obedience. This, too, takes time.

We intentionally pursue God by putting the disciplines in our
schedules and expecting him to work through them. As his Spirit
taps us on the shoulder and tells us we're off track, we respond

with humility, "Yes, Lord, I repent. Lead me and strengthen me. I choose to make better choices next time." As we pursue God, the Spirit works in our hearts and minds to gradually transform us. The interval between the Spirit's conviction and our repentance grows shorter, and our love for Christ grows stronger. Bad habits are gradually replaced by good and godly disciplines, and sometimes, as gifts from God, we are surprised by God's work in and through us. When that happens, we are delighted—and so is God—by the changes he brings.

RICH REWARDS

As I look back on my years of walking with God, I can see that he's taken me through all kinds of circumstances to build my faith. Quite often, the faith-builders were answers to prayer, people coming to Christ, the Holy Spirit's touch and comfort in times of need, and a million other manifestations of the grace of God. But sometimes God took me through times of disappointment and doubt when I didn't sense his presence and I had no clue what direction to take. But looking back, I can see that those, too, were steppingstones of growth for my family and me.

The longer I walk with God, the more I treasure his word. It's a gold mine of truth, encouragement, insight, and challenge. I can read a passage I've read hundreds of times, and God often illuminates my heart to grasp the truth at a deeper level. That's thrilling to me! I love to then teach other people what I've learned, and they seem to benefit from it. That, too, is a great joy to me.

Wisdom comes from many sources. We can learn valuable lessons vicariously as we watch other people make dumb mistakes and avoid them ourselves. We can read the directives of law in the Bible and see the prohibitions as protection. And we can associate with mature men and women who can impart the life of Christ as they walk with us through good times and bad.

I've made plenty of dumb mistakes in my years of walking with God, but he has given me friends who have believed in me, challenged me, and run along side me. I know what David felt like when Saul wanted to kill him and Jonathan became his best friend. Those friends in my life have meant, and continue to mean, the world to me. Sure, we've had disagreements, but in a trusting relationship, that's part of the joy of life. We can disagree without becoming critical. In that way, we sharpen each other, and our love, trust, and respect keep growing.

I used to be a very driven person. I'm still too much like that, but walking with God for these years has mellowed me at least a little. (Just ask Elaine.) I used to believe that I had to achieve certain things to be acceptable to people and to God. The drive itself wasn't wrong, but the focus was off base. Now, I'm just as driven, but not as much to win approval and achieve prestige. By God's great grace, I care a bit more now about his honor than mine, and building his kingdom instead of building one for me.

In many ways, growing in Christ is narrowing our focus from the wide range of the world's values, day by day, step by step, to finally get to the one we need the most: Jesus. The writer to the Hebrews tells us, "Therefore, since we are surrounded by such a great cloud of witnesses, let us throw off everything that hinders and the sin that so easily entangles, and let us run with perseverance the race marked out for us. Let us fix our eyes on Jesus, the author and perfecter of our faith, who for the joy set before him endured the cross, scorning its shame, and sat down at the right hand of the throne of God. Consider him who endured such opposition from sinful men, so that you will not grow weary and lose heart" (Hebrews 12:1-3).

The "witnesses" are believers who are with Christ today, watching us from the stands in heaven, cheering us on. Think about that: Right now, millions of people who experienced the same joys and struggles you and I face are watching us and rooting for us! That's encouraging.

The writer tells us to throw aside anything and everything that hinders us in our long race in the Christian life. Throughout this book, we've identified all kinds of things that can hinder us: the love of money, comparing ourselves and our possession with others, a sense of shame, pride, and Satan's lies, to name a few. Now we fix our gaze on Jesus. He has already run his race, and it was a lot tougher than anything you and I have to face. We may be tempted to give up and quit, but as we think about his example, we'll choose to hang in there and trust God one more day, for the rest of our lives.

And at the end, when we've trusted God through the good times and bad, and even though we've wavered and been confused at times, we will stand before Jesus and he'll say those wonderful words, "Well done, good and faithful servant. Enter into the joy of your Master." And that will be enough.

As long as I am alive on earth, I want to respond to Christ's invitation as he calls to me through each of the seven doors of spiritual growth. The adventure of walking with him is amazing, and he assures me again and again that he's not finished doing wonderful things in me and through me. The best, I'm sure, is yet to come. And on that day when I see him face to face and he welcomes me home, the best will then have come!

> **The adventure of walking with him is amazing, and he assures me again and again that he's not finished doing wonderful things in me and through me.**

THINK ABOUT IT

1. Think about Jesus' story about the two houses in Matthew 7. What does the sand symbolize? What are some types of storms, wind, and waves that show if our houses are built on rock or sand? On a scale of 0 (not at all) to 10 (completely), how much is your life built on the rock? How can you tell?

2. Look at Psalm 51. Does the thought of being completely honest and humble about your sins frighten you or free you? Explain your answer.

3. Describe characteristics of each stage of spiritual growth: child, adult, and parent. Which one best represents you at this point in your spiritual journey? (If no one were listening to you or watching over your shoulder as you write, how would you answer that question?) Does this realization encourage you or discourage you? Explain your answer.

4. Now that you've finished this book, what is the next step for you? What are the three most important things you need to do to continue to grow in your relationship with Christ? Who or what will help you keep growing?

GOING DEEPER

1. Review the passages and quotes in the section titled "The Hard Road." What insights did you gain from this section? What difference would it make for you to believe that God's "grace is sufficient for you" in the hardest times in your life?

2. Which of the rewards mentioned is most attractive to you? Explain your answer.

3. What have you learned about God's grace in your study of this book? What have you learned about your willingness and ability to embrace grace? What have you learned about your willingness and ability to extend grace to others?

Endnotes

1   Larry Crabb, *Finding God,* (Zondervan, Grand Rapids, 1993), p. 18.

2   Dr. Karl Menninger, *Whatever Became of Sin?,* (Hawthorn Books, New York, 1973), p. 13.

3   Philip Yancey, *Reaching for the Invisible God,* (Zondervan, Grand Rapids, 2000), pp. 255-256.

4   C. F. W. Walther, translated by Herbert J. A. Bouman, *Law and Gospel,* (CPH, St. Louis, 1959), p. 14.

5   *Luther's Works,* American Edition, Vol. 23, p. 270ff.

6   Rick Warren, "Living By Grace" a message given on September 11-12, 1999, www.pastors.com

7   "Luther's Small Catechism," Concordia Publishing House, 1986, pp. 17-18.

8   Ibid., pp. 19-20.

9   Ibid., p. 15.

10 Ibid., p. 6.

11 Os Guinness, *The Call,* (Word, Nashville, 1998), p. 4.

12 Ibid., p. 47.

13 Adapted from a newsletter by Iris Lowder, 1998.

14 Caedmon's Call, "Carry Your Love," *In the Company of Angels.*

15 John Ortberg, "Diagnosing Hurry Sickness," *Leadership,* Fall, 1998.

15 www.helpguide.org/mental/burnout_signs_symptoms.htm

16 Dietrich Bonhoeffer, *Cost of Discipleship,* (The MacMillan Company, New York: 1963), p. 17.

17 Robert Lewis, *The Quest for Authentic Manhood,* (LifeWay, Nashville, 2003).

18 Yancey, *Reaching for the Invisible God,* p. 115.

19 Francis de Sales, *The Art of Loving God,* (Manchester, N.H.: Sophia Institute, 1998), p. 36.

20 Yancey, *Reaching for the Invisible God,* p. 143.

21 "Luther's Small Catechism," p. 3.

22 Randy Alcorn, *Heaven,* (Tyndale House Publishers, Wheaton, Illinois, 2004), p. 17.

23 www.sima4nonprofit.com

24 "The State of Church Giving Through 2003" (Fifteenth edition, 2005).

25 Yancey, *Reaching for the Invisible God,* pp. 211-246.

26 Jean-Pierre de Caussade, *The Sacrament of the Present Moment,* (Harper San Francisco, San Francisco, 1989), p. 72.

27 J. I. Packer, *Knowing God,* (Intervarsity Press, Downer's Grove, 1973), p. 227.

About the Author

John H. Kieschnick was born in Walburg, Texas, on March 5, 1942, as the second youngest of nine children. He attended Lutheran schools in Walburg and San Antonio, Texas, and he went to high school and junior college at Concordia Academy and Junior College in Austin, Texas. He received a B.S. in Education from Concordia Teachers College in River Forest, Illinois, in 1964.

In the first part of his career, Kieschnick served as teacher, principal, and youth director at Calvary Lutheran Church and Day School in Havertown, Pennsylvania, from 1964 to 1966. In 1966, God called him to the pastoral ministry, so he entered Concordia Theological Seminary in Springfield, Illinois. He completed his vicarage at Jehovah Lutheran Church, Chicago, Illinois. He received his B.D. from the seminary in May 1970, and his M.Div. in May 1985.

Kieschnick's first pastoral call was accepted to Our Redeemer Lutheran Church in Irving, Texas. He was ordained and installed at the church on August 9, 1970, and served there until October 1974.

Since October of 1974, Pastor Kieschnick has served as Senior Pastor of Gloria Dei Lutheran Church in Houston (Nassau Bay), Texas. During this time, the church has grown from 400 to more than 3200 baptized members, with an average weekend attendance exceeding 1700. The church has undergone six capital campaigns and building programs, and is now preparing for its seventh campaign under his pastorate. This major capital stewardship program will fund the new multi-site ministry of Gloria Dei, initially extending into North Galveston County. At Gloria Dei, God has used Kieschnick, his staff, and lay leaders to develop a strong ministry in support of its mission, *"to reach out and help people experience a growing relationship with Jesus Christ and His church."*

Pastor Kieschnick served as an elected Board of Parish Services member for the Texas District of the Lutheran Church – Missouri Synod from 1972 to 1982. He was responsible for the Stewardship of Giving Committee. During these years, he served as the Texas District Director for the Synod's 125th Anniversary Thankoffering, developed annual stewardship programs, and authored a "Christian Money Management Program." He also served as primary author and editor for the District's "Stewards In His Service" program.

In addition, Pastor Kieschnick served as a Circuit Counselor for several years. He served on the District's Church Growth Task Force and on the national board of the Lutheran Church Extension Fund, St. Louis, from 1988 to 1998. He served as a founding member of the Pastoral Leadership Institute Board of Directors.

Presently, Kieschnick is a member of the Board of Regents of Concordia Theological Seminary in Fort Wayne, Indiana, his alma mater. He frequently consults with congregations regarding planning, management, leadership, and stewardship.

Kieschnick married Elaine Trimble on July 4, 1970, and they have been blessed with three children: Jonathan, Kimberly, and Jason. He enjoys "dreaming dreams" and "seeing visions," and he "plays at" golf in his spare time.

HOW TO LEAD A GROUP
OR CLASS USING
The Best Is Yet to Come

This book is designed for individual study and small groups. The most powerful way to absorb and apply these principles is for each person to study and consider the application questions individually and then discuss them in either a class or a group environment.

The questions at the end of each chapter are designed to promote reflection, discussion, and application. Most groups meet weekly, but some may need to meet every other week. If your group meets weekly, use all seven questions ("Think About it" and "Going Deeper") at the end of each chapter. If your group meets every other week, focus on the first four questions ("Think About It") at the end of the chapters. Regardless of how often your group meets, begin and end each session with a time of prayer.

Get copies of the book to group members the week before the series begins so they will be ready to discuss the Introduction.

For those that meet weekly, a recommended schedule is:

Week 1	Introduce the material. Walk through the Table of Contents. Have each individual complete the Spiritual Health Awareness Survey, which can be found on page 233 of this appendix. (You are encouraged and have permission to copy the Survey for use in your group.) Have participants share insights from their surveys and discuss their hopes for the group. Cover the questions at the end of the Introduction.
Weeks 2–9	Cover Chapters 1–8.
Week 10	Cover Chapter 9 of the book. Have the members of the group take the Spiritual Health Awareness

Survey again and discuss the results and plans for continued growth.

For those groups that meet every other week, a recommended schedule is:

Session 1   Introduce the material. Walk through the Table of Contents. Have each individual complete the Spiritual Health Awareness Survey, which can be found on page 233 of this appendix. (You are encouraged and have permission to copy the Survey for use in your group.) Have participants share insights from their surveys and discuss their hopes for the group. Cover the questions at the end of the Introduction.

Session 2   Cover Chapters 1 and 2.

Session 3   Cover Chapters 3 and 4.

Session 4   Cover Chapters 5 and 6.

Session 5   Cover Chapters 7 and 8.

Session 6   Cover Chapter 9. Have the members of the group take the Spiritual Health Awareness Survey again and discuss the results and plans for continued growth.

Order enough books for each person to have a copy. For couples, encourage both to have their own book so they can record their individual thoughts and prayers.

PERSONALIZE EACH LESSON

Make sure you personalize the principles and applications. At least once in each group meeting, add your own story, either a success or a failure, to illustrate a particular point. Make the Scriptures come alive. For instance, if you are using a passage from the gospels, put your group in the scenes with Pharisees scowling, sinners rejoicing, and disciples often confused. Far too often, we read the Scriptures like a phone book, with little or no emotion. Paint a vivid picture for people. Provide insights about the context of the encounters with Jesus, and help people sense the emotions of specific people in each scene.

FOCUS ON APPLICATION

This book is written to help people experience God's grace so their lives are transformed. Make sure you ask the "Think About It" questions each week. As time permits tackle one or more of the "Going Deeper" questions. Allow ample time to discuss these! Share how you are applying the principles in the chapter, and encourage them to take steps of growth, too.

THREE TYPES OF QUESTIONS

If you have led groups for a few years, you already understand the importance of using open questions to stimulate discussion. Three types of questions are *limiting, leading,* and *open.*

- *Limiting questions* focus on an obvious answer, such as, "What does Jesus call himself in John 10:11?" These don't stimulate reflection or discussion. If you want to use questions like this, follow them with thought-provoking open questions.

- *Leading questions* sometimes require the listener to guess what the person asking has in mind, such as, "Why did Jesus use the metaphor of a shepherd in John 10?" (He was probably alluding to a passage in Ezekiel, but most people wouldn't know that.) The teacher who asks a leading question has a definite answer in mind. Instead of asking this question, he should teach the point and perhaps ask an open question about the point he has made.

- *Open questions* usually don't have right or wrong answers. They stimulate thinking, and they are far less threatening because the person answering doesn't risk ridicule for being wrong. These questions often begin with "Why do you think…?" or

"What are some possible reasons that…?" or "How would you have felt in that situation?"

PREPARATION

1. As you prepare to teach this material in a group, consider these steps:

2. Order books at least two weeks before the class begins.

3. Carefully and thoughtfully read the book. Make notes, highlight key sections, quotes, or stories, and personally respond to the questions at the end of each chapter. This will familiarize you with the entire scope of the content.

4. As you prepare for each lesson, read the corresponding chapter again and make any additional notes.

5. Tailor the amount of content to the time allotted. You may not have time to cover all the questions, so pick the ones that are most pertinent.

6. Add your own stories to personalize the message and add impact.

7. Before and during your preparation, ask God to give you wisdom, clarity, and power. Trust him to use your group to change people's lives.

8. Most people will get far more out of the group if they read a chapter of the book each week.

The Best Is Yet to Come

A SPIRITUAL HEALTH AWARENESS SURVEY

INTRODUCTION

Jesus made it very clear to his disciples, "You did not choose me, but I chose you and appointed you to go and bear fruit – fruit that will last. Then the Father will give you whatever you ask in my name. This is my command: Love each other." (John 15:16-17)

While the words appear clear enough, what exactly do they mean? How do I know if I am bearing "fruit"? Jesus said, "Love each other," but how do I measure my "love"? Christians have wrestled with these questions for centuries, and there are no precise answers.

However, as we look at the early Christian church in Jerusalem at Pentecost and shortly thereafter, as recorded in Acts 2:37-47, we begin to see evidences of that fruit and manifestations of that love. At Gloria Dei, we have identified seven of these and called them "disciplines," which we believe are evidences of fruit and love in the lives of followers of Jesus. These seven disciplines are the focus of this book. We have tried to make it clear that these disciplines do not begin with us, but are rooted in grace, that is, they begin with God and end with him. Those who follow Jesus are his disciples and are the conduits or instruments through whom the grace of God is to flow back to him.

In order to help you determine how effectively God's grace is flowing through you, this survey is provided for your use. Please *do not use it as a test*. If you do, you will either feel too bad or too good about yourself. Rather, use it as an inventory, an instrument for spiritual self-awareness, and then ask God to continue to shower his grace in and through you with the confidence that *"the best is yet to come!"*

Circle the number which best represents your spiritual health. (You may wish to repeat this inventory in the future to do additional "check ups.")

1—*Not at all/Never*

2—*Not much/Rarely*

3—*Somewhat/Occasionally*

4—*Mostly/Often*

5—*Always/Completely*

WITNESS

Growing followers of Jesus are witnesses and they witness because they have experienced the witness of God's grace in Jesus. (Acts 1:8; 2:38-41; 22:14-16)

1. I witness Christ to all in what I say.   1 2 3 4 5
2. I witness Christ to all by what I do.   1 2 3 4 5
3. I am able to clearly explain what I believe   1 2 3 4 5
   and why.
4. I regularly pray for those who do not know   1 2 3 4 5
   Jesus as Savior and Lord.

WORSHIP

Growing followers of Jesus worship God because they have experienced their true worth in him. (Acts 2:42c; 46a and 47b; Psalm 100)

1. I seek to worship God seven days a week,   1 2 3 4 5
   24 hours a day.
2. I faithfully attend weekly worship of God with   1 2 3 4 5
   my fellow believers.
3. I seek to worship God by surrendering   1 2 3 4 5
   everything in my life to him.
4. I experience the on-going presence of God   1 2 3 4 5
   more and more each day.

CONNECTION

Growing followers of Jesus connect with God and one another in the church because they have first been connected to him by grace through faith in Christ. (Acts 2:42b, 44, 46b; Hebrews 10:19-25)

1. I cherish my connection with God by grace through faith in Jesus.   1 2 3 4 5
2. I participate actively in a small group that helps me grow in my faith.   1 2 3 4 5
3. I build deep relationships with people God gives to me.   1 2 3 4 5
4. I allow others to hold me accountable for my growth as a Christian.   1 2 3 4 5

PRAYER

Growing followers of Jesus commune with God in prayer because they have first heard his word of grace spoken to them. (Acts 2:42d; Luke 11:1-4)

1. I pray more or less constantly, both listening to God and speaking to him.   1 2 3 4 5
2. I pray "continually" on a daily basis.   1 2 3 4 5
3. I enter God's presence with awe, humility, gratitude, and expectancy.   1 2 3 4 5
4. I find my prayer life effective and rewarding.   1 2 3 4 5

BIBLE STUDY

Growing followers of Jesus examine the Scriptures regularly because they have first experienced his word of judgment and grace to them. (Acts 2:42a; 17:10-12)

1. I find great delight in reading the Bible daily on my own.   1 2 3 4 5
2. I like to learn from others by studying the Bible in a group.   1 2 3 4 5
3. I examine the Bible to determine what is right and what is wrong.   1 2 3 4 5

4. I study the Bible so that I can become   1 2 3 4 5
   more Christ-like.

SERVICE

Growing followers of Jesus serve God and others because they
have first experienced God's service to them in Christ. (Acts
2:43; 1 Peter 4:7-11)

1. I see my entire life as one of service to God   1 2 3 4 5
   and others.
2. I have discovered my unique Spirit-given shape   1 2 3 4 5
   for ministry.
3. I serve in a ministry of my church to help   1 2 3 4 5
   build up the body of Christ.
4. I actively seek opportunities to serve others   1 2 3 4 5
   in my community.

GIVING

Growing followers of Jesus give of their financial resources because they have first experienced the evidences of God's grace to
them in these resources. (Acts 2:45; 2 Corinthians 8:7)

1. I believe everything I have is a gift of God's   1 2 3 4 5
   grace to me.
2. I seek to manage 100% of my resources in   1 2 3 4 5
   line with God's word.
3. I give at least a tenth (a tithe) of my income   1 2 3 4 5
   to support the church.
4. I acquire my wealth ethically and pay my   1 2 3 4 5
   taxes honestly.

A FEW QUESTIONS FOR YOU TO CONSIDER

1. In which disciplines did you score the higher numbers?

    — What do you enjoy about these aspects of your walk with Christ?

    — What do you need to do to excel still more?

2. In which disciplines did you score lower marks?

    — What or who are some resources to help you walk more closely with Christ in these areas?

    — What is your plan to make specific changes?

"WHERE DO I GO FROM HERE?"

Taking a survey such as this one can stir up a variety of feelings within us. While we may feel very good about certain disciplines in our lives, we also know we have a long way to go. This produces feelings of inadequacy, and possibly, even shame. What are we to do with these responses? The Biblical word repentance provides the answer. We are to confess our sins and shortcomings and lay them at the foot of the cross of Jesus. Then, we are to receive his forgiveness. This is why Jesus died on the cross. Finally, as forgiven sinners, we are set free to commit ourselves to be transformed. We can change! That's the good news of God's grace to us in Jesus. We can become more Christ-like. And in the process, God will help his church grow.

Take King David's words to heart and make them your prayer. He wrote, "Trust in the Lord and do good; dwell in the land and enjoy safe pasture. Delight yourself in the Lord and he will give you the desires of your heart. Commit your way to the Lord; trust in him and he will do this: He will make your righteousness shine like the dawn, the justice of your cause like the noonday sun" (Psalm 37:3-6).

Finally, look to the future with great confidence. Because of God's grace in Christ, it really is true: "The best is yet to come!"

TO ORDER MORE COPIES OF
The Best Is Yet to Come

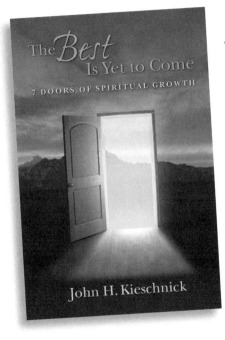

This book can be used by individuals, groups, classes, or leadership teams. Use it as a foundation for rich reflection and stimulating discussion. Books also make great gifts for all occasions.

To order more copies and for information about discounts and shipping...

Go online to: www.gdlc.org and click on "resources."

Or write to:　　*The Best Is Yet to Come*
　　　　　　　　Gloria Dei Lutheran Church
　　　　　　　　18220 Upper Bay Road
　　　　　　　　Houston, TX 77058-4198

Payment options: Credit cards are accepted online. Checks are accepted by mail.